PAUL FIGLEY

A Guide to the
Federal Tort
Claims Act

SECOND EDITION

ABA
SECTION OF
ADMINISTRATIVE LAW
AND REGULATORY
PRACTICE

Cover design by Amanda Fry/ABA Design

Printed in the United States of America.

22 21 20 19 18   5 4 3 2 1

ISBN: 978-1-64105-291-7
e-ISBN: 978-1-64105-292-4

Library of Congress Cataloging-in-Publication Data

Names: Figley, Paul, author. | American Bar Association. Section of
   Administrative Law and Regulatory Practice, sponsoring body.
Title: A guide to the Federal Tort Claims Act / edited by Paul Figley.
Description: Second edition. | Chicago : American Bar Association, [2018] |
   Includes bibliographical references and index.
Identifiers: LCCN 2018039185 | ISBN 9781641052917 (print) |
   ISBN 9781641052924 (epub)
Subjects: LCSH: United States. Federal Tort Claims Act. | Government
   liability—United States. | United States—Claims.
Classification: LCC KF1321 .F54 2018 | DDC 342.7308/8—dc23
LC record available at https://lccn.loc.gov/2018039185

www.ShopABA.org

Contents

To Marty—who earns royalties on all her books

About the Author

Paul Figley was a litigator in the Civil Division of the U.S. Department of Justice for three decades, much of that time working on Federal Tort Claims Act issues. For fifteen years he served as Deputy Director, Torts Branch, where his responsibilities included the defense of many of the cases discussed in this book. He now teaches Torts and Legal Rhetoric at American University's Washington College of Law. There, he was twice elected Professor/Faculty Member of the Year by the Student Bar Association and, in 2017, received the Emalee C. Godsey Award for faculty scholarship. The author would like to thank Emily Brait, Patricia Fitzgerald, Lauren Goldschmidt, Joseph Gross, Kimberly Harding, Adeen Postar, and Catherine Warren for their research assistance.

Foreword

Paul Figley had a decades-long career litigating and managing Federal Tort Claims Act (FTCA) issues at the Department of Justice, much of the time serving as the Deputy Director of the office responsible for most governmental tort claims and litigation. His depth of knowledge of the FTCA is well-known. Paul's clarity of presentation and straightforward analysis is legendary. He has outdone himself in this gem of a guide.

Acts or omissions on the part of federal government officers and employees regularly result in injuries to others due to carelessness or wrongful conduct under circumstances where the usual remedy is a claim for monetary damages to compensate the injured person—a tort claim. Tort claims against the federal government must begin and proceed in accordance with the FTCA. This book is an invaluable guide to understanding whether and how to pursue an FTCA remedy. Similarly, government attorneys will find this book to be of substantial assistance whenever they consider FTCA issues.

The FTCA was carefully drafted to balance special federal interests with the need for a fair tort remedy. Several substantial sets of amendments expanded the rights initially enacted and, in other respects, narrowed the rights available. The Act must be examined with care to gain an appreciation of its metes and bounds, which are sometimes remarkably different from the usual tort claimant's expectations. This is not to say that the FTCA is a trap for the unwary; rather, it is to say that a lawyer well-versed in tort law needs to understand pertinent provisions of the FTCA in order to represent his or her client effectively. This guide is exactly what any attorney needs to provide counsel on torts arising from the federal government's enormous range of activities.

Jeffrey Axelrad

Jeffrey Axelrad is an Adjunct Professor at George Washington University Law School. He was with the United States Department of Justice from 1967 to 2003, serving as Chief, Torts Section and then Director of the Torts Branch's FTCA Staff from 1977 to 2003.

CHAPTER 1

Introduction

This book is intended to provide a concise overview of the Federal Tort Claims Act (FTCA) and its jurisprudence. The presentation here is simplified so it can be quickly read and easily understood.[1] The book should be useful to attorneys or law-trained readers who are new to the FTCA and its procedures or have had limited recent dealings with the statute. It should also provide a ready reference for readers of all levels who are about to begin detailed research on particular FTCA issues. The book is an outline rather than a complete exposition of FTCA jurisprudence. There are nuances to almost every FTCA issue that are worthy of more detailed research.

The book addresses the FTCA's waiver of sovereign immunity, its purpose,[2] scope, exclusions,[3] exceptions,[4] and the procedures for presenting administrative tort claims[5] and filing suit.[6] It discusses the protections the FTCA may provide to federal employees sued in tort.[7]

---

1. An in-depth analysis of the FTCA and related issues is provided in the excellent three-volume treatise, LESTER S. JAYSON & ROBERT C. LONGSTRETH, HANDLING FEDERAL TORT CLAIMS (2018).

2. Chapter 2. Sovereign Immunity & Enactment of the FTCA.

3. Chapter 3. The Limited Nature of the FTCA's Waiver of Sovereign Immunity: A. The Jurisdictional Grant of § 1346(b)(1); B. The *Feres* Doctrine.

4. Chapter 4. Statutory Bars to FTCA Liability: A. Exceptions in the Text of the FTCA; B. Statutes That Explicitly Bar Suit; C. Other Statutes That Bar Suit.

5. Chapter 5. The Administrative Claims Process: Procedural Prerequisites to Making a Tort Claim.

6. Chapter 6. Procedural Requirements in FTCA Litigation: A. Exhaustion of Administrative Remedies; B. Courts, Juries, & Parties; C. The FTCA's Statutes of Limitations.

7. Chapter 7. Government Employee Defendants & the FTCA: A. Substitution & Dismissal under § 2679; B. The Judgment Bar of § 2676.

It explains the FTCA's rules for damages[8] and for financial matters, including attorney's fees, costs, and interest.[9] Finally, it examines the FTCA settlement process and recommends approaches to settlement negotiations.[10]

The Appendix includes the FTCA,[11] federal statutes relating to interest, costs, and payment;[12] the federal regulations on FTCA administrative claims, certification of scope of employment, authority to compromise, and representation of federal employees.[13] It provides a copy of Standard Form 95 (for submission of FTCA administrative claims)[14] and information for filing a Transcript of Judgment (a necessary step to obtain interest on an FTCA judgment).[15] It includes

---

8. Chapter 8. Damages: A. Assessing Damages; B. Amount Stated in Administrative Claim; C. No Punitive Damages; D. Accounting for Taxes in FTCA Damages; E. No Pre-Judgment Interest.

9. Chapter 9. Source of Payment, Attorney's Fees, Costs, and Interest: A. Source of Payment; B. Attorney's Fees; C. Costs; D. Interest.

10. Chapter 10. Settlement.

11. Appendix A. Federal Tort Claims Act.
   28 U.S.C. § 1346(b)(1). United States as defendant [Jurisdiction].
   28 U.S.C. § 1402(b). United States as defendant [Venue].
   28 U.S.C. § 2401(b). Time for commencing action against United States.
   28 U.S.C. § 2402. Jury trial in actions against United States.
   28 U.S.C. § 2671 *et seq.* Tort Claims Procedures.

12. Appendix B. Judgments, Costs, Interest.
   28 U.S.C. § 1961. Interest.
   28 U.S.C. § 2412. Costs and fees.
   28 U.S.C. § 2414. Payment of judgments and compromise settlements.
   28 U.S.C. § 2516 Interest on Claims and Judgments.
   31 U.S.C. § 1304. Judgments, awards, and compromise settlements.

13. Appendix C. Regulations.
   28 C.F.R. Part 14—Administrative Claims Under Federal Tort Claims Act.
   28 C.F.R. Part 15—Certification and Decertification in Connection with Certain Suits Based upon Acts or Omissions of Federal Employees and Other Persons.
   28 C.F.R. Part 0, Subpart Y—Authority to Compromise and Close Civil Claims and Responsibility for Judgments, Fines, Penalties, and Forfeitures.
   28 C.F.R. Part 50.15—Representation of Federal officials and employees by Department of Justice attorneys or by private counsel furnished by the Department in civil, criminal, and congressional proceedings in which Federal employees are sued, subpoenaed, or charged in their individual capacities.

14. Appendix D. Standard Form 95.

15. Appendix E. Filing Transcript of Judgment.
   1. Contact information: Financial Management Service, Judgment Fund Branch.
   2. Sample letter filing Transcript of Judgment.

checklists for FTCA defenses,[16] filing an administrative claim,[17] and filing an FTCA suit.[18]

The book focuses on the FTCA. Accordingly, it does not address non-tort defenses the government might raise in FTCA litigation such as the State Secrets privilege,[19] the Political Question doctrine,[20] and the rule adopted in *Totten v. United States* barring suits based on espionage agreements.[21] Nor does it address actions brought against individual federal employees under *Bivens v. Six Unknown Named Agents of Fed. Bureau of Narcotics*,[22] other than to note the procedures by which such employees can request representation from the Department of Justice.[23]

---

16. Appendix F. Checklist of FTCA Defenses.

17. Appendix G. Checklist for Filing Administrative Tort Claim.

18. Appendix H. Checklist for Filing FTCA Suit.

19. *See* United States v. Reynolds, 345 U.S. 1, 7–11 (1953).

20. *See* El-Shifa Pharm. Indus. Co. v. United States, 607 F.3d 836, 842–44 (D.C. Cir. 2010); *see also* Baker v. Carr, 369 U.S. 186 (1962).

21. Totten v. United States, 92 U.S. 105 (1876) (suit by Civil War spy); *see* Tenet v. Doe, 544 U.S. 1, 3 (2005) (applying rule established in *Totten*, "prohibiting suits against the Government based on covert espionage agreements").

22. Bivens v. Six Unknown Named Agents of Fed. Bureau of Narcotics, 403 U.S. 388 (1971).

23. *See* page 60, *infra*.

CHAPTER 2

Sovereign Immunity & Enactment of the FTCA

The doctrine of sovereign immunity provides that a sovereign state can be sued only to the extent that it has consented to be sued and that only its legislative branch can give such consent.[1] The federal government cannot be sued for damages unless Congress has enacted an applicable waiver of the United States' sovereign immunity.[2] "A waiver of the Federal Government's sovereign immunity must be unequivocally expressed in statutory text, . . . and will not be implied. . . ."[3] Accordingly, the default position is that no one can sue the United States in tort unless Congress has passed a statute waiving the government's sovereign immunity for such a suit.[4] The

---

1. *See, e.g.*, United States v. Dalm, 494 U.S. 596, 610 (1990) (stating that a central principle to our understanding of sovereign immunity is Congress' reservation of the power to consent); United States v. U.S. Fid. & Guar. Co., 309 U.S. 506, 514 (1940) ("Consent alone gives jurisdiction to adjudge against a sovereign. Absent that consent, the attempted exercise of judicial power is void. . . . Public policy forbids the suit unless consent is given, as clearly as public policy makes jurisdiction exclusive by declaration of the legislative body.").

2. United States v. Testan, 424 U.S. 392, 399 (1976) (quoting United States v. Sherwood, 312 U.S. 584, 586 (1941)) ("Thus, except as Congress has consented to a cause of action against the United States, 'there is no jurisdiction . . . in any . . . court to entertain suits against the United States.'"); United States v. McLemore, 45 U.S. 286, 288 (1846) ("[T]he government is not liable to be sued, except with its own consent, given by law."); *see also* Cohens v. Virginia, 19 U.S. 264, 411–12 (1821) ("The universally received opinion is, that no suit can be commenced or prosecuted against the United States; that the judiciary act does not authorize such suits.").

3. Lane v. Pena, 518 U.S. 187, 192 (1996) (citing United States v. Nordic Vill., Inc., 503 U.S. 30, 33–34, 37 (1992); Irwin v. Dep't of Veterans Affairs, 498 U.S. 89, 95 (1990)); *accord* United States v. U.S. Fid. & Guar. Co., 309 U.S. 506, 514 (1940) ("Consent alone gives jurisdiction to adjudge against a sovereign. . . . Public policy forbids the suit unless consent is given, as clearly as public policy makes jurisdiction exclusive by declaration of the legislative body.").

4. *See Lane*, 518 U.S. at 192.

5

Federal Tort Claims Act provided a general waiver for tort cases when it became law in 1946.[5]

From the founding of the Republic until 1946 the chief recourse for citizens injured by the torts of federal employees was to ask Congress to enact private legislation affording them relief.[6] The right to seek such legislation is grounded in the Constitution,[7] but Congress is poorly suited to adjudicate liability issues.[8] As John Quincy Adams reasoned:

> [Deciding private claims] is judicial business, and legislative assemblies ought to have nothing to do with it. One-half of the time of Congress is consumed by it, and there is no common rule of justice for any two of the cases decided. A deliberative assembly is the worst of all tribunals for the administration of justice.[9]

Members of Congress had long shared that view and objected to their involvement with private claims.[10] By the Twentieth Century, congressional procedures for addressing private claims were well

---

5. Pub. L. No. 79-601, ch. 753, Title IV, 60 Stat. 842 (codified in scattered sections of 28 U.S.C.).

6. *See Hearings on H.R. 5373 and H.R. 6463 Before H. Comm. on the Judiciary*, 77th Cong, 2d Sess., at 24–25 (statement of Ass't Att'y Gen. Francis M. Shea) (1942) [hereinafter *Hearings on H.R. 5373 and H.R. 6463*]; James E. Pfander & Jonathan L. Hunt, *Public Wrongs and Private Bills: Indemnification and Government Accountability in the Early Republic*, 85 N.Y.U. L. Rev. 1862, 1888–92 (2010); *see also* Lester S. Jayson & Robert C. Longstreth, Handling Federal Tort Claims § 2.01 (2018) (noting that private legislation "was a tortuous and frequently hopeless route to recovery").

7. U.S. Const. amend. I.; *see* Paul Fredric Kirgis, *Section 1500 and the Jurisdictional Pitfalls of Federal Government Litigation*, 47 Am. U. L. Rev. 301, 302 (1997) (citing Wilson Cowen et al., The United States Court of Claims, A History, Part II: Origin-Development-Jurisdiction, 1855–1978, at 9 (1978)).

8. *See, e.g., Hearings on H.R. 5373 and H.R. 6463, supra* note 6, at 39–41.

9. *Id.* at 49 (internal quotation marks omitted). Similarly, Abraham Lincoln said, "The investigation and adjudication of claims in their nature belong to the judicial department." *Id.* at 46 (citing First Annual Message to Congress, December 3, 1861; Congressional Globe, 37th Cong., 2d sess. Pt III, appendix, pp. 1, 2).

10. *See Hearings on H.R. 5373 and H.R. 6463, supra* note 6, at 49–55 (comments dating from 1832 to 1941 by congressmen criticizing the private claims bills system).

established but remarkably inefficient.[11] The process was subject to interminable delays and arbitrary actions.[12] Congress was not able to efficiently decide tort claims on their merits.[13]

Considering and evaluating claims was a substantial burden on the time and attention of Congress.[14] Service on the Committee on Claims was considered onerous "not only because of the number of claims submitted but because of the realization that careful judicial consideration of the claims is for the most part impossible."[15] Committee members simply could not know the details of each of the thousands of claims presented in every Congress.[16] Proposals for a general tort claims act were debated for decades.[17] Finally, the 79th Congress enacted the FTCA as Title IV of the Legislative Reorganization Act of 1946,[18] which President Truman signed into law

---

11. In 1926, the House of Representatives procedure for enacting such a private bill called for the claim to be referred to the Committee on Claims. *See Hearings on H.R. 5373 and H.R. 6463, supra* note 6, at 51 (citing H.R. REP. No. 69-667, at 18 (1926) (Supplementary Report of Rep. Emanuel Celler)). If the committee took favorable action, the claim would be forwarded to the House where it would be placed on the Private Calendar. *Id.* Any member could strike it from that calendar for any reason. *Id.*

12. *Hearings on H.R. 5373 and H.R. 6463, supra* note 6, at 54 (statement of Rep. Luce) (noting the waste of time and inequity of procedures and stating that "nothing is so disgraceful in the conduct of the Congress of the United States as its treatment of claims").

13. *See id.* at 49–55. The House Report also quotes the 1926 statement of Massachusetts Rep. Charles L. Underhill:

> The power vested in the chairman of the Committee on Claims is tremendous and absolutely wrong. I can either refuse arbitrarily to consider your claim or I can take up each and every one of your claims to suit my convenience. . . .
>
> I have one case that has passed five different Congresses, one branch or the other, and has failed of passage in both branches the same year, not because it did not have justification but because it was too late; it got caught in the jam; it could not get through; and these claimants have been waiting all of these years for relief in the payment of a debt which the United States owes them.

Id. at 52 (citing 67 CONG. REC. 7,526 (1926)).

14. *See, e.g.,* S. REP. No. 79-1400, at 30–31 (1946); H.R. REP. No. 79-1287, at 2 (1945); *Hearings on H.R. 5373 and H.R. 6463, supra* note 6, at app. II, 49–55 ("Criticisms by Congressmen of Existing Procedure of Relief by Private Claim Bills").

15. *See* H.R. REP. No. 79-1287, at 2 (1945).

16. *See Hearings on H.R. 5373 and H.R. 6463, supra* note 6, at 54 (quoting *Debates on H.R. 7236*, 86 CONG. REC. 18212 (1940)).

17. *See generally id.* at 49–55; JAYSON & LONGSTRETH, *supra* note 6, § 2.09–.10.

18. Pub. L. No. 79-601, 60 Stat. 812 (codified as amended in scattered sections of 28 U.S.C.).

on August 2, 1946.[19] Title I of the Legislative Reform Act prohibited Congress from considering private bills regarding matters that might be paid under the FTCA.[20]

The background to the FTCA provides four important lessons for practitioners new to this area. First, the doctrine of sovereign immunity is the law of the land.[21] Suits directly challenging it are almost certain to fail.[22] Second, the FTCA defines the scope of the United States' liability in tort. Artful pleading cannot be used to avoid the limits, defenses, and exclusions of the FTCA.[23] The meaning "of a term used in the FTCA 'is by definition a federal question.'"[24] Third, Congress does not want to deal with individual tort claims. By statute it has barred itself from considering any private bill "for which suit may be instituted under the [FTCA]. . . ."[25] Accordingly, until a claim

---

19. Harry S. Truman, Statement by the President Upon Signing the Legislative Reorganization Act (Aug. 2, 1946), *reprinted in* 92 CONG. REC. 10,675 (1946).

20. Pub. L. No. 79-601, 60 Stat. 812. The pertinent section reads:

> SEC. 131. No private bill or resolution (including so-called omnibus claims or pension bills), and no amendment to any bill or resolution, authorizing or directing (1) the payment of money for property damages, for personal injuries or death for which suit may be instituted under the [FTCA] . . . shall be received or considered in either the Senate or the House of Representatives.

21. *See supra* text at notes 1–4. Sovereign immunity does not bar suits against federal employees for Constitutional torts or certain claims made under the Takings Clause of the Fifth Amendment; U.S. CONST. amend. V.; Bivens v. Six Unknown Named Agents of Fed. Bureau of Narcotics, 403 U.S. 388, 396 (1971). Other waivers of sovereign immunity may provide relief where the FTCA does not. *See, e.g.*, The Suits in Admiralty Act, 46 U.S.C. §§ 741–752; The Death on the High Seas Act, 46 U.S.C. §§ 761–768; The Public Vessels Act, 46 U.S.C. §§ 781–790; the Tucker Act, 28 U.S.C. §§ 1346(a), 1491.

22. *See, e.g.*, U.S. Dep't of Army v. Blue Fox, Inc., 525 U.S. 255, 261 (1999) (explaining that waiver of sovereign immunity is strictly construed in favor of the sovereign (citing Lane v. Pena, 518 U.S. 187, 192 (1996))); United States v. Nordic Vill., Inc., 503 U.S. 30, 33–34 (1992) (noting waivers of sovereign immunity must be "unequivocally expressed").

23. *See* United States v. Shearer, 473 U.S. 52, 55 (1985) (plurality opinion) ("No semantical recasting of events can alter the fact that the battery was the immediate cause of [the injury] and consequently, the basis of respondent's claim."); *accord* United States v. Neustadt, 366 U.S. 696, 703 (1961).

24. Dry v. United States, 235 F.3d 1249, 1257 (10th Cir. 2000) (quoting Molzof v. United States, 502 U.S. 301, 305 (1992)); *see Neustadt*, 366 U.S. at 705–06 ("Whether or not this analysis [of 'misrepresentation'] accords with the law of States which have seen fit to allow recovery under analogous circumstances, it does not meet the question of whether this claim is outside the intended scope of the Federal Tort Claims Act, which depends solely upon what Congress meant by the language it used in § 2680(h).").

25. *See* Pub. L. No. 79-601, § 131, *supra* note 20.

has been fully litigated under the FTCA there is no point in seeking relief from Congress.[26] Even then, a positive legislative outcome is unlikely. Fourth, Congress does want valid tort claims against the government to be adjudicated and paid, so long as they fall within the scope of claims Congress authorized when it enacted the FTCA.

---

26. *See generally id.*

CHAPTER 3

The Limited Nature of the FTCA's Waiver of Sovereign Immunity

A. The Jurisdictional Grant of § 1346(b)(1)

When Congress granted United States district courts subject matter jurisdiction to hear FTCA suits, it defined the scope of its waiver of sovereign immunity in the jurisdictional grant.[1] In *Federal Deposit Insurance Corp. v. Meyer*, the Supreme Court confronted the issue whether the FTCA waived the United States' sovereign immunity for constitutional torts.[2] To resolve that issue the *Meyer* Court dissected the language of the jurisdictional grant:

> Section 1346(b) grants the federal district courts jurisdiction over a certain category of claims for which the United States

---

1. 28 U.S.C. § 1346(b)(1) (2012):

   Subject to the provisions of chapter 171 of this title, the district courts, together with the United States District Court for the District of the Canal Zone and the District Court of the Virgin Islands, shall have exclusive jurisdiction of civil actions on claims against the United States, for money damages, accruing on and after January 1, 1945, for injury or loss of property, or personal injury or death caused by the negligent or wrongful act or omission of any employee of the Government while acting within the scope of his office or employment, under circumstances where the United States, if a private person, would be liable to the claimant in accordance with the law of the place where the act or omission occurred.

2. 510 U.S. 471, 477 (1994). *Meyer* was brought by a former employee of a failed savings and loan association who was discharged, allegedly in violation of his due process right to property (continued employment), by the government agency which acted as receiver of the institution. *Id.*

has waived its sovereign immunity and "render[ed]" itself liable. This category includes claims that are:

"[1] against the United States, [2] for money damages, . . . [3] for injury or loss of property, or personal injury or death [4] caused by the negligent or wrongful act or omission of any employee of the Government [5] while acting within the scope of his office or employment, [6] under circumstances where the United States, if a private person, would be liable to the claimant in accordance with the law of the place where the act or omission occurred." 28 U.S.C. § 1346(b).

A claim comes within this jurisdictional grant–and thus is "cognizable" under § 1346(b)–if it is actionable under § 1346(b). And a claim is actionable under § 1346(b) if it alleges the six elements outlined above.[3]

This analysis effectively explains why courts lack subject matter jurisdiction over claims that do not fall within the precise language of the jurisdictional grant.[4] Claims not encompassed by the language of § 1346(b) are excluded from the FTCA's general waiver of sovereign immunity.[5] The Court held that Meyer's constitutional tort claim alleging violation of his due process right to property (continued employment) was not cognizable under the FTCA because a private person would not be liable on such a claim under state law.[6]

The first three elements of § 1346(b) are straightforward and can be briefly addressed. Simply put, the FTCA cannot be used to

---

3. *Id.* at 477 (internal citations omitted).

4. *Id.* at 475 ("Sovereign immunity is jurisdictional in nature.").

5. *See id.* at 477–79; *see also* United States v. Olson, 546 U.S. 43, 46 (2005) (recognizing that § 1346(b)(1) waives the United States' sovereign immunity under circumstances where a private person would be liable (rather than as a state or municipal entity would be liable) and that the Court had consistently adhered to the "private person" standard).

6. 510 U.S. at 477–78 (citing 28 U.S.C. § 1346(b)).

sue any person or entity other than the United States.[7] The only remedy available under the FTCA is "money damages,"[8] and then only for claims "for injury or loss of property, or personal injury or death . . . ."[9] The other elements of § 1346(b) have received more attention.

Because the jurisdictional grant is for torts arising from a "negligent or wrongful act or omission,"[10] the FTCA does not support claims for strict or absolute liability. For example, the Supreme Court held that suits arising from sonic booms do not fall within the FTCA.[11] Likewise, claims alleging strict liability for blasting[12] or other ultra-hazardous activity are barred,[13] as are claims arising under strict

---

7. *See, e.g.*, Smith v. United States, 561 F.3d 1090, 1099 (10th Cir. 2009) ("The United States is the only proper defendant in an FTCA action."); Johnson v. V.A. Med. Ctr., 133 F. Supp. 3d 10, 17 (D.D.C. 2015) (dismissing action for failure to name the proper party, but granting leave to amend to substitute the United States as defendant).

8. *See, e.g.*, Janis v. United States, 162 Fed. Appx. 642, 643–44 (7th Cir. 2006) (holding the FTCA would not support injunction prisoner sought "to stop prison officials and employees from hindering . . . plaintiff from redressing his grievances").

9. *See, e.g.*, Idaho *ex rel.* Trombley v. U.S. Dep't of Army, 666 F.2d 444, 446 (9th Cir. 1982) (barring state's claim for firefighting costs because they were not "for injury or loss of property"); Oregon v. United States, 308 F.2d 568, 569 (9th Cir. 1962) (same); California v. United States, 307 F.2d 941, 944 (9th Cir. 1962) (same).

10. 28 U.S.C. § 1346(b)(1).

11. *See* Laird v. Nelms, 406 U.S. 797, 798 (1972) (citing § 1346(b)) (holding that because the jurisdictional grant is for claims for a "negligent or wrongful act or omission," claims for strict or absolute liability cannot be brought under the FTCA); Peak v. Small Bus. Admin., 660 F.2d 375, 378 (8th Cir. 1981) ("The holding in *Laird* did not indicate that such claims are not governed by the provisions of the FTCA, but simply that they are barred by the provisions of the FTCA. The practical effect . . . is the same as if Congress had included it as an exemption under Section 2680.").

12. *See, e.g.*, *Laird*, 406 U.S. at 800 ("the presently prevailing view as to the theory of liability for blasting damage is frankly conceded to be strict liability for undertaking an ultrahazardous activity").

13. *See* Lively v. United States, 870 F.2d 296, 300 (5th Cir. 1989) (affirming dismissal of strict liability claim for asbestos sale; "it is clear that strict liability 'no fault' claims are not cognizable under the FTCA").

liability dram shop acts,[14] and state statutes modeled on §402A of the Restatement (Second) of Torts.[15]

For the FTCA to apply, the "negligent or wrongful act or omission" must be that of an "employee of the Government."[16] Accordingly, the FTCA does not cover the torts of employees of the District of Columbia,[17] territorial governments,[18] or a VA physician's fiancée on a house-hunting trip in a new city.[19] The issue of federal employment generally turns on whether a common law master-servant relationship exists with the federal government.[20] State or local law

---

14. *See* Miller v. United States, 463 F.3d 1122, 1125 (10th Cir. 2006) (affirming dismissal "because the exclusive vehicle for recovery against a dram shop in Utah is governed by a strict liability statute under which the plaintiff need not establish negligence, such action is not within the scope of the FTCA's immunity waiver").

15. *See In re* All Maine Asbestos Litigation, 581 F. Supp. 963, 972 (D. Me. 1984):

> There is no doubt that the Maine statute upon which Count II is based, 14 M.R.S.A. §221 (1980), is a strict liability statute. Adams v. Buffalo Forge Co., 443 A.2d 932, 934–44 (Me. 1982). *See* Restatement (Second) of Torts §402A (1965) and Comment a. Consequently, Count II does not state a claim over which this Court has jurisdiction under the FTCA.

See also In re Bomb Disaster at Roseville, 438 F. Supp. 769, 771 (E.D. Cal. 1977) (barring strict liability and 402A claims arising from explosion of eighteen boxcars carrying government bombs).

16. 28 U.S.C. §1346(b)(1). The FTCA defines "Employee of the government" to include:

> (1) officers or employees of any federal agency, members of the military or naval forces of the United States, members of the National Guard while engaged in training or duty under section 115, 316, 502, 503, 504, or 505 of title 32, and persons acting on behalf of a federal agency in an official capacity, temporarily or permanently in the service of the United States, whether with or without compensation, and (2) any officer or employee of a Federal public defender organization, except when such officer or employee performs professional services in the course of providing representation under section 3006A of title 18.

17. Cannon v. United States, 645 F.2d 1128, 1137 (D.C. Cir. 1981); Jordan v. District of Columbia, 113 F. Supp. 3d 278, 281 (D.D.C. 2015) (mayor of D.C. not a federal employee).

18. Harris v. Boreham, 233 F.2d 110, 166 (3d Cir. 1956) (finding that a Virgin Islands maintenance supervisor is not government employee under the FTCA).

19. Brandes v. United States, 783 F.2d 895 (9th Cir. 1986), *reversing* 569 F. Supp. 538, 543 (N.D. Cal. 1983).

20. *See* Lester S. Jayson & Robert C. Longstreth, Handling Federal Tort Claims §§ 2.01, 8.04 (2018) ("A servant is a person employed to perform services in the affairs of another and who with respect to the physical conduct in the performance of the services is subject to the other's control or right of control." (citing Restatement (Second) of Agency §220(1))).

enforcement officers deputized as federal officers[21] may be federal employees for FTCA purposes and entitled to its statutory immunity for common law torts.[22] Other defendant-tortfeasors who do not fall obviously within the "[e]mployee of the government" definition, including informants,[23] inspectors,[24] jurors,[25] and private agencies,[26] have sought to be treated as federal employees for FTCA purposes.[27]

---

21. *See, e.g.,* 5 U.S.C. §3374. Assignments of employees from state or local governments.

22. *See, e.g.,* Provancial v. United States, 454 F.2d 72, 75 (8th Cir. 1972) (holding city police officers with special commission to arrest Indians within Indian Reservation were federal employees for FTCA purposes); Chin v. Wilhelm, 291 F. Supp. 2d 400, 403 (D. Md. 2003) (holding Baltimore City Police officers assigned to DEA Task Force were federal employees for FTCA purposes), *aff'd,* No. 06-1428, 2006 U.S. App. LEXIS 32075 (4th Cir. Dec. 29, 2006).

23. Wang v. United States, 947 F.2d 1400, 1401 (9th Cir. 1991) (remanding case for determination whether Internal Revenue Service informant should be certified as a federal employee for FTCA purposes). *Compare* Leaf v. United States, 661 F.2d 740, 741 (9th Cir. 1981) (holding DEA informant who rented airplane for use in undercover operation was federal employee for FTCA purposes), *with* Slagle v. United States, 612 F.2d 1157, 1160 (9th Cir. 1980) (holding DEA informant involved in shooting was not federal employee under FTCA).

24. *Compare* Haddix v. Yetter Mfg. Co., 209 F. Supp. 2d 915, 916 (N.D. Ill. 2002) (holding Occupational Safety and Health Administration inspector was not a federal employee), *with In re* Air Crash Disaster near Silver Plume, 445 F. Supp. 384, 400 (D. Kan. 1977) (holding FAA inspector was a federal employee).

25. Sellers v. United States, 672 F. Supp. 446, 449 (D. Idaho 1987) (holding prospective juror driving to courthouse was not a federal employee).

26. Daniels v. Liberty Mut. Ins. Co., 484 F.3d 884, 885 (7th Cir. 2007) (industry anti-fraud organization, the National Insurance Crime Bureau, unsuccessfully sought to be certified as federal employee for FTCA purposes).

27. There is also a significant question whether a corporation can be deemed to be a federal employee for FTCA purposes. *Compare* Adams v. United States, 420 F.3d 1049, 1050 (9th Cir. 2005) (holding that helicopter company retained to spread herbicide could not be certified as a federal employee because "the word 'persons' as used in this portion of the FTCA does not include corporations"), *and* Vallier v. Jet Propulsion Lab., 120 F. Supp. 2d 887, 893 (C.D. Cal. 2000) (rejecting request by university engaged in rocket research that it be certified as federal employee for FTCA purposes), *aff'd in unpublished opinion,* 23 F. App'x 803 (9th Cir. 2001), *with* B&A Marine Co., Inc. v. Am. Foreign Shipping Co., 23 F.3d 709, 714–15 (2d Cir. 1994) (holding that the American Foreign Shipping Company was a federal employee because, *inter alia,* its contract with the Maritime Administration "expressly provided that AFS would serve 'as [the Maritime Administration's] agent, and not as an independent contractor'").

As a general matter, the FTCA does not apply to torts of government contractors.[28] The Supreme Court recognized in *Logue v. United States*,[29] where a federal prisoner committed suicide while housed in a county jail, that a contractor may be deemed a federal employee if the government controls the detailed physical aspects of its operations.[30] The Court held that the contractor exclusion applied in *Logue* because the United States had "no authority to physically supervise the conduct of the jail's employees," although the contract required the county to follow Bureau of Prisons' "standards of treatment for federal prisoners, including methods of discipline, rules for communicating with attorneys, visitation privileges, mail, medical services, and employment . . . ."[31] In some jurisdictions, the United States may be liable for the torts of a contractor if the claim is based on a non-delegable duty.[32] By statute Congress has decreed that the FTCA (including its procedures and defenses) is the exclusive remedy for certain torts of nuclear weapons contractors, 50 U.S.C. § 2783, tribal employees or contractors, Pub. L. No. 101-512, Title III, § 314, 104 Stat. 1915, 1959 (1990) (codified at 25 U.S.C. § 450f note), and Community Health Center personnel, 42 U.S.C. § 233.

---

28. The FTCA defines the term "Federal agency" as including "the executive departments, the judicial and legislative branches, the military departments, independent establishments of the United States, and corporations primarily acting as instrumentalities or agencies of the United States, *but does not include any contractor with the United States.*" 28 U.S.C. § 2671 (emphasis added).

29. Logue v. United States, 412 U.S. 521, 530 (1973).

30. *Id.* at 527; *see* United States v. Orleans, 425 U.S. 807, 817 (1976) (holding community service agency was not a federal agency even though it received federal funding and complied with federal regulations).

31. *Logue*, 412 U.S. at 530. In both *Orleans* and *Logue* the Supreme Court cited the RESTATEMENT (SECOND) OF AGENCY § 2 (1958). *Orleans*, 425 U.S. at 815, n.4; *Logue*, 412 U.S. at 528 n.5.

32. *Compare* Dickerson, Inc. v. United States, 875 F.2d 1577, 1582–84 (11th Cir. 1989) (deciding that the United States was liable under the FTCA for negligent transport of PCBs by a contractor because Florida law imposed a non-delegable duty), *with* Roditis v. United States, 122 F.3d 108, 111–12 (2d Cir. 1997) (per curiam) (dismissing FTCA claim of plaintiff who fell on a Post Office construction site maintained by a contractor because the New York non-delegable duty to maintain premises would be a form of strict liability).

Since the jurisdictional grant limits the waiver of sovereign immunity to torts of federal employees "acting within the scope of [their] office or employment," the FTCA does not apply to acts or omissions that are outside the scope of employment.[33] Whether a federal employee is acting within the scope of employment turns on the respondeat superior law of the state in which the wrongful act or omission occurred.[34] This brings into play the common issues of state law regarding respondeat superior liability, including whether the act was incidental to the employee's responsibilities,[35] was intended to further the employer's interests,[36] or was within the time and space limits of the employment.[37] It also involves special issues such as

---

33. 28 U.S.C. § 1346(b)(1).

34. Williams v. United States, 350 U.S. 857, 857 (1955) (per curiam) ("This case is controlled by the California doctrine of respondeat superior."), *vacating* 215 F.2d 800, 808 (9th Cir. 1954) (affirming dismissal because negligent acts of a soldier while off duty and off base were outside military line of duty).

35. *See, e.g.*, Council on American Islamic Relations v. Ballenger, 444 F.3d 659, 662, 664–66 (D.C. Cir. 2006) (per curiam) (finding that a Congressman's phone interview with a reporter from a newspaper in his home district discussing his marriage in which he referred to plaintiff as a "fundraising arm for Hezbollah" was incidental to his responsibilities); Meridian Int'l Logistics, Inc. v. United States, 1994 WL 395866, at *1–2 (9th Cir. July 28, 1994) (finding that FBI agent was acting in a way that was "broadly incidental" to his employment when he made allegedly tortious statements about plaintiff).

36. *See, e.g.*, Taboas v. Mlynczak, 149 F.3d 576, 582 (7th Cir. 1998) (holding that defendant's allegedly defamatory statements about supervisor's mental stability were motivated, at least in part, by employer's interest in maintaining a safe workplace); Aversa v. United States, 99 F.3d 1200, 1211 (1st Cir. 1996) (finding that Assistant U.S. Attorney's allegedly tortious statements regarding plaintiff's involvement in a money laundering scheme were intended, at least in part, to further the Department of Justice's interests).

37. *See, e.g.*, Tonelli v. United States, 60 F.3d 492, 495 (8th Cir. 1995) (finding that a postal worker who opened and photocopied plaintiffs' adult-oriented mail was not acting within the time and space of his employment). *But see* Vollendorff v. United States, 951 F.2d 215, 218–19 (9th Cir. 1991) (holding that Army pilot who kept government-required medication in his home, which was subsequently ingested by a child causing permanent damage, was acting within the time and space of his employment).

frolic and detour,[38] the going and coming rule,[39] and the special mission rule.[40]

The jurisdictional grant applies only to wrongful acts or omissions "under circumstances where the United States, if a private person, would be liable to the claimant in accordance with the law of the place where the act or omission occurred."[41] Like a private person, the United States can be sued for contribution "not only in a separate proceeding but also as a third-party defendant."[42] But Congress did not create new causes of action when it enacted the FTCA.[43] Rather, the Act incorporates the existing and evolving tort law of the states[44] and their conflicts of law rules.[45] Moreover, the United States' liabil-

---

38. *See, e.g.,* Mider v. United States, 322 F.2d 193, 197 (6th Cir. 1963) (holding two soldiers were on a frolic; "[t]hey took the government vehicle to go to [soldier's] home for an entirely personal weekend frolic, and became intoxicated on the way, and, before the collision which occurred fifty-five miles from the Base.").

39. *See, e.g.,* Clamor v. United States, 240 F.3d 1215, 1217 (9th Cir. 2001) (holding that Navy civilian employee who had auto accident in government rented vehicle while leaving work for the day was not acting within the scope of his employment under Hawaii law). *But see* Healy v. United States, 435 F. Supp. 2d 157, 163 (D.D.C. 2006) (holding that FBI agent driving from home to work was within scope of employment under D.C. law because his use of FBI car served the agency's needs).

40. *See, e.g.,* Smollen v. United States, 46 F.3d 65 (5th Cir. 1995) (per curiam) (finding that although Department of Energy employee was in Houston on a special mission generally, he was not acting within the scope of his employment when his car hit a pedestrian after a personal meeting).

41. 28 U.S.C. § 1346(b)(1); *see* United States v. Olson, 546 U.S. 43, 45–46 (2005); Rayonier, Inc. v. United States, 352 U.S. 315, 318 (1957) (holding that United States is liable to the same extent as a private person for negligence pertaining to forest fires); Indian Towing Co. v. United States, 350 U.S. 61, 64–65 (1955) (reasoning that once the government undertook to maintain a lighthouse it can be liable for its negligent operation under the FTCA like a private person in a good Samaritan situation who undertakes to help but does so negligently).

42. United States v. Yellow Cab Co., 340 U.S. 543, 551, 556–57 (1951).

43. Feres v. United States, 340 U.S. 135, 142 (1950) ("[The FTCA's] effect is to waive immunity from recognized causes of action and was not to visit the Government with novel and unprecedented liabilities.").

44. Indian Towing Co. v. United States, 350 U.S. 61, 68 (1955) ("The broad and just purpose which the statute was designed to effect was to compensate the victims of negligence in the conduct of Governmental activities in circumstances like unto those in which a private person would be liable."); *see also* George W. Conk, *Will the Post 9/11 World Be a Post-Tort World?*, 112 PENN ST. L. REV. 175, 247 (2007) (discussing the Swine Flu campaign by the government to provide vaccine for the anticipated Swine Flu epidemic, and stating "the Federal Tort Claims Act retains vitality and that it incorporates the flexibility of underlying state common law").

45. *See* Richards v. United States, 369 U.S. 1, 11, 12–13. (1962).

ity is like that of a private person, not of a state or municipality.[46] This means that there is no FTCA subject matter jurisdiction unless the case involves a tort under state law.[47] If there is no actionable duty under state law against a private person, there can be no tort claim against the United States.[48] Accordingly, if private parties do not engage in analogous activity, there is no analogous private person liability, and the waiver of sovereign immunity does not apply.[49] Likewise, if a private person cannot be sued in tort for violation of a federal statute or regulation, then the government cannot be sued in tort for such a violation. For example, in *Art Metal-USA, Inc. v. United States*, the D.C. Circuit affirmed dismissal of an action alleging that the General Services Administration negligently failed to follow its own procurement regulations when it refused to approve government contracts with the plaintiff.[50] The court held that violation of a federal statute or regulation cannot form the basis of an FTCA suit: "[B]y basing its negligence claim entirely on violation of federal duties, [plaintiff] fails to consider that the FTCA waives the immunity

---

46. *See* United States v. Olson, 546 U.S. 43, 46 (2005).

47. *See, e.g.*, Delta Sav. Bank v. United States, 265 F.3d 1017, 1025–26 (9th Cir. 2001) (finding there is no subject matter jurisdiction because plaintiff bank could not point to any liability arising under California law); Williams v. United States, 242 F.3d 169, 177 (4th Cir. 2001) (holding the United States is not liable for Native American hospital's failure to provide emergency care to non-Indian because there was no duty to do so under state tort law).

48. *See, e.g.*, Walters v. United States, 474 F.3d 1137, 1141 (8th Cir. 2007) (finding that the United States was not liable for an accident that occurred as a result of loose gravel on a roadway because a private party would have no duty to prevent such a condition); Pate v. Oakwood Mobile Homes, Inc., 374 F.3d 1081, 1084 (11th Cir. 2004) (holding that there is no analogous duty of private parties to insure that OSHA violations are abated).

49. *See* United States v. Agronomics, Inc., 164 F.3d 1343, 1346 (10th Cir. 1999) (barring suit against Federal Mine and Health Safety Administration for adverse financial repercussions of an administrative determination because such a function is not something a private person can undertake); C.P. Chem. Co. v. United States, 810 F.2d 34, 37–38 (2d Cir. 1987) (affirming dismissal of suit by insulation manufacturer that went out of business after the Consumer Product Safety Commission banned the type of insulation it manufactured); Jayvee Brand, Inc. v. United States, 721 F.2d 385, 390 (D.C. Cir. 1983) (affirming dismissal of suit by pajama manufacturers challenging ban on flame retardant; "quasi-legislative or quasi-adjudicative action by an agency of the federal government is action of the type that private persons could not engage in and hence could not be liable for under local law. Thus, there is here no jurisdiction to entertain a suit against the federal government.").

50. Art Metal-USA, Inc. v. United States, 753 F.2d 1151, 1157 (D.C. Cir. 1985).

of the United States only to the extent that a private person in like circumstances could be found liable in tort under local law."[51]

On a more mundane level, any defense that is available under state law to a private person defendant is available to the United States in an FTCA suit. These defenses include contributory negligence,[52] comparative negligence,[53] superseding cause,[54] assumption of risk,[55] recreational use statutes,[56] and the statutory employer doctrine.[57]

---

51. *Id.* at 1157 (emphasis in original). *See, e.g.*, *Delta Sav. Bank*, 265 F.3d at 1024–25 ("Plaintiffs suggest, without support, that an FTCA claim can be brought for violations of federal statutes that provide private federal causes of action, even if there is no analogous state law. This is not so.").

52. *See, e.g.*, Kahn v. United States, 795 F. Supp. 473, 476 (D.D.C. 1992) (finding contributory negligence where plaintiff stepped into Kennedy Center elevator car that was two feet lower than the floor); Allnutt v. United States, 498 F. Supp. 832, 844 (W.D. Mo. 1980) (finding contributory negligence where pilot struck power line while flying below one hundred feet); Craft v. United States, 237 F. Supp. 717, 719 (E.D.S.C. 1965) (finding contributory negligence where plaintiff sat on folding checkerboard table that collapsed).

53. *See, e.g.*, Murff v. United States, 785 F.2d 552, 555 (5th Cir. 1986) (barring suit where airplane pilots' negligence exceeded that of air traffic controllers; "[t]he Texas form of comparative negligence permits no recovery against one who is less negligent than the plaintiff." (citing Article 2212a, Tex. Rev. Civ. Stat. § 1)); Yeary v. United States, 754 F. Supp. 546, 553 (E.D. Mich. 1991) (applying Michigan's pure comparative negligence standard in pedestrian-postal vehicle case, court reduced damages by forty percent); Walton v. United States, 484 F. Supp. 568, 576 (S.D. Ga. 1980) (applying Georgia comparative negligence standard in lost burial vault case, court granted no recovery because plaintiff's fault exceeded government's).

54. Ins. Co. of N. Am. v. United States, 527 F. Supp. 962, 971 (E.D. Ark. 1981) (finding for United States because superseding negligence of airplane pilot caused crash).

55. *See, e.g.*, Clem v. United States, 601 F. Supp. 835, 845 (N.D. Ind. 1985) (applying Indiana "incurred risk doctrine" where swimmer entered unfamiliar waters after being informed no lifeguard was present and the waters were hazardous); Mullins v. Blackwell, 283 F. Supp. 462, 463 (N.D. Ga. 1967) (assumption of risk doctrine barred suit by federal prisoner struck by baseball while spectator at game).

56. *See, e.g.*, Matheny v. United States, 469 F.3d 1093, 1096 (7th Cir. 2006) (finding that the Indiana Recreational Use Statute foreclosed recovery by woman who was injured by a protruding pipe while sled-riding in a national park); Wilson v. United States, 989 F.2d 953, 959 (8th Cir. 1993) (holding that the Missouri Recreational Use Statute protected the United States from liability for a Boy Scout's death while on government-owned lands).

57. *See, e.g.*, Vega-Mena v. United States, 990 F.2d 684, 688 (1st Cir. 1993) (finding that the United States was the plaintiff's statutory employer under the Puerto Rico Workman's Compensation Act, meaning that the United States was not liable in tort for injuries the plaintiff sustained after falling into a vat of diesel fuel waste); Leigh v. Nat'l Aeronautics and Space Admin., 860 F.2d 652, 653 (5th Cir. 1988) (holding that the Louisiana statutory employer doctrine protected the United States from liability for injuries employee of a subcontractor sustained while testing the external tank of the space shuttle).

B. The *Feres* Doctrine

The "private person liability" element is also the root of the *Feres* doctrine which holds that "the Government is not liable under the Federal Tort Claims Act for injuries to servicemen where the injuries arise out of or are in the course of activity incident to service."[58] In *Feres*, the Supreme Court examined the FTCA and concluded that Congress had not intended to waive sovereign immunity for injuries that arise incident to military service.[59] The Court explained, "We do not think that Congress, in drafting this Act, created a new cause of action dependent on local law for service-connected injuries or death due to negligence."[60]

Whether *Feres* applies to a particular claim turns on whether the injury arose incident to military service.[61] In determining that issue courts consider a variety of factors, with no single one being dispositive.[62] Important factors in resolving whether an injury arose incident to service include the following: whether the injury arose

---

58. Feres v. United States, 340 U.S. 135, 141 (1950):

> One obvious shortcoming in these claims is that plaintiffs can point to no liability of a "private individual" even remotely analogous to that which they are asserting against the United States. We know of no American law which ever has permitted a soldier to recover for negligence, against either his superior officers or the Government he is serving.

59. *Id.* at 146.

60. *Id.* In the *Feres* opinion, the Court discussed three rationales for the proposition that, when it enacted the FTCA, Congress did not intend to waive sovereign immunity for suits by servicemen against the United States: (1) the absence of private person liability, *id.* at 141; (2) the availability of a separate, uniform, comprehensive, no-fault compensation scheme to military personnel, *id.* at 145; and (3) the distinctly Federal relationship between the government and members of the Armed Forces, and the corresponding unfairness of permitting service incident claims to be determined by non-uniform local law, *id.* at 142–44. For further discussion of the *Feres* doctrine, see Paul Figley, *In Defense of Feres: An Unfairly Maligned Opinion*, 60 AM. U. L. REV. 393 (2011).

61. United States v. Johnson, 481 U.S. 681, 686 (1987) (barring claim asserting service member killed in helicopter crash caused by FAA civilian employee's negligence; "[t]his Court has never deviated from [the incident to service test] of the *Feres* bar.").

62. Richards v. United States, 176 F.3d 652, 655 (3d Cir. 1999).

while a service member was on active duty;[63] whether the injury arose on a military situs;[64] whether the injury arose during a military activity;[65] whether the service member was taking advantage of a privilege or enjoying a benefit conferred as a result of military service when the injury arose;[66] and whether the injury arose while the service member was subject to military discipline or control.[67] If the injury arose out of activity incident to service suit is barred regardless of whether the claim is filed for the injuries to the U.S. servicemember,[68] for injuries to a foreign servicemember,[69] for

---

63. *See* Kohn v. United States, 680 F.2d 922, 925 (2d Cir. 1982) (*Feres* barred claim of soldier shot by fellow soldier); Chambers v. United States, 357 F.2d 224, 227 (8th Cir. 1966) (*Feres* barred claim of airman drowned in base swimming pool).

64. *See* Morey v. United States, 903 F.2d 880, 881 (1st Cir. 1990) (*Feres* barred claim of sailor falling off pier on return to ship); Millang v. United States, 817 F.2d 533, 534–35 (9th Cir. 1987) (*Feres* barred claim of off-duty marine run over by on-duty MP on military installation). *But see* Dreier v. United States, 106 F.3d 844, 852 (9th Cir. 1996) (ruling that "the situs of his injury is not determinative.").

65. *See* Costo v. United States, 248 F.3d 863, 869 (9th Cir. 2001) (*Feres* barred suit by family members of sailors who drowned while participating in Navy-led recreational rafting trip); Galligan v. City of Phila., 156 F. Supp. 2d 467, 474 (E.D. Pa. 2001) (*Feres* barred claim of West Point cadet injured while watching Army-Navy football game).

66. *See* Quintana v. United States, 997 F.2d 711, 712 (10th Cir. 1993) (*Feres* barred medical malpractice claim by National Guard member who was performing inactive duty for training when she injured her knee and subsequently received medical treatment at Air Force hospital while off duty); Herreman v. United States, 476 F.2d 234, 237 (7th Cir. 1973) (*Feres* barred claim of soldier hitching ride on military aircraft while on leave).

67. *See* Pringle v. United States, 208 F.3d 1220, 1226–27 (10th Cir. 2000) (*Feres* barred claim of soldier injured when ejected from on-base social club under the operational control of base commander); Stewart v. United States, 90 F.3d 102, 104 (4th Cir. 1996) (*Feres* barred claim of soldier injured in on-post automobile accident while returning to quarters after mandatory physical training).

68. *See* Dozler v. United States, 869 F.2d 1165, 1166 (8th Cir. 1989) (per curiam) (*Feres* barred claim for wrongful death of soldier murdered in Army barracks); Ordahl v. United States, 601 F. Supp. 96, 99 (D. Mt. 1985) (*Feres* barred suit by serviceman who was struck in the eye by a dart fired from fellow serviceman's blowgun while in Air Force barracks).

69. *See* Daberkow v. United States, 581 F.2d 785, 788 (9th Cir. 1978) (*Feres* barred suit by West German pilot killed while on training flight); Aketepe v. United States, 925 F. Supp. 731, 737 n.2 (M.D. Fla. 1996) (*Feres* barred suit by Turkish sailors injured when their destroyer was struck by live missiles fired from United States carrier during naval exercise), *aff'd on other grounds*, 105 F.3d 1400 (11th Cir. 1997).

loss of consortium by the servicemember's spouse,[70] or on a third party indemnity against the United States for payments made to an injured servicemember.[71]

By the same token, *Feres* does not bar claims of veterans that arise after they have left military service.[72] But it does apply to claims that arise when a service member is injured incident to service and alleges a post-service injury from another tort, such as a failure to warn or provide follow-up care.[73] *Feres* does not bar a servicemember from suing for injuries to a spouse or family member so long as those injuries were not incurred "incident to service."[74] If injuries to a child have their genesis in injuries to a service member, the injuries are

---

70. *See* Skees v. United States, 107 F.3d 421, 424–25 (6th Cir. 1997) (*Feres* barred widow's loss of consortium claim after Army failed to prevent husband's suicide); De Font v. United States, 453 F.2d 1239, 1240 (1st Cir. 1972) (*Feres* barred derivative claim from serviceman's widow for mental anguish permitted under Puerto Rican law).

71. Stencel Aero Eng'g Corp. v. United States, 431 U.S. 666, 673–75 (1977) (*Feres* barred Government contractor from seeking indemnity for damages paid to National Guard pilot injured by plane's escape hatch system).

72. United States v. Brown, 348 U.S. 110, 112 (1954) ("The injury was not incurred while [Brown] was on active duty or subject to military discipline. The injury occurred after his discharge, while he enjoyed a civilian status."); M.M.H. v. United States, 966 F.2d 285, 288 (7th Cir. 1992) (*Feres* doctrine did not bar claim for negligence in post discharge suicide).

73. Lombard v. United States, 690 F.2d 215, 221 (D.C. Cir. 1982) (alleging post-discharge duty to warn of dangers of in-service exposure to radiation); Laswell v. Brown, 683 F.2d 261, 267 (8th Cir. 1982) (same). *But cf.* Maas v. United States, 94 F.3d 291, 296–98 (7th Cir. 1996) (finding similar claim not barred by *Feres*, but barred by discretionary function).

74. Hicks v. United States, 368 F.2d 626, 633 (4th Cir. 1966) (serviceman may recover for wrongful death of civilian wife after treatment in military hospital); Costley v. United States, 181 F.2d 723, 726 (5th Cir. 1950) (*Feres* does not bar claim for wrongful death of wife); Phillips v. United States, 508 F. Supp. 544, 550 (D.S.C. 1981) (sailor and wife could recover for "wrongful birth" of son).

incident to service and suit is barred by *Feres*.[75] *Feres* does not bar obstetrical malpractice claims if the negligent medical care was provided to the fetus or newborn child rather than to its service member mother.[76]

A second, much less frequently used body of *Feres* jurisprudence arises from the decision in *United States v. Shearer* in which an Army private was kidnapped and murdered by another private who previously had been convicted of manslaughter but retained in the service.[77] It bars FTCA suits brought for injuries to servicemembers, which are "the *type* of claims that, if generally permitted, would involve the judiciary in sensitive military affairs at the expense of military discipline and effectiveness."[78] It applies to claims such as those which go "directly to the 'management' of the military; [that] call into question basic choices about the discipline, supervision and control of a serviceman."[79] The test here does not focus on the injured servicemember, but on the nature of the challenged activity; suit is barred when a service member's injury allegedly arises from core military decisions or the management of other members of the

---

75. Ortiz v. United States, 786 F.3d 817, 841 (10th Cir. 2015) (barring plaintiff's *in utero* injuries that arose from its servicemember mother's blood pressure problems); Ritchie v. United States, 733 F.3d 871, 873 (9th Cir. 2013) (barring plaintiff's *in utero* injuries allegedly caused when servicemember mother was required to perform "battle-focused PT . . . even if she did not feel up to it"); Minns v. United States, 155 F.3d 445, 450 (4th Cir. 1998) (barring suit for birth defects allegedly caused by parents' exposure to drugs and chemicals in Gulf War); Lombard v. United States, 690 F.2d 215, 223 (D.C. Cir. 1982) (father exposed to ionizing radiation during nuclear weapons test); Scales v. United States, 685 F.2d 970, 973 (5th Cir. 1982) (servicemember mother allegedly exposed to rubella vaccine).

76. *See* Brown v. United States, 462 F.3d 609, 614 (6th Cir. 2006) (holding *Feres* did not bar claim where medical care was provided directly to the fetus); Romero v. United States, 954 F.2d 223, 227 (4th Cir. 1992) (same); *cf.* Irvin v. United States, 845 F.2d 126, 127 (6th Cir. 1988) (holding *Feres* barred claim that government negligently provided prenatal care); Del Rio v. United States, 833 F.2d 282, 287–88 (11th Cir. 1987) (holding *Feres* barred claim for death of son who died five days after birth, but not claim of twin brother who survived with brain damage).

77. United States v. Shearer, 473 U.S. 52 (1985).

78. *Id.* at 59 (emphasis by Court).

79. *Id.* at 58.

military.[80] The *Shearer* analysis arose in the setting of an assault by one service member upon another[81] and it is most frequently applied in that context.[82]

---

80. *See, e.g.*, Mackey v. United States, 226 F.3d 773, 776 (6th Cir. 2000) (*Feres* applied to FTCA sexual harassment suit brought by Air Force captain); Pringle v. United States, 208 F.3d 1220, 1227 (10th Cir. 2000) (*Feres* applied to soldier's challenge to decisions regarding management of NCO club); Skees v. United States, 107 F.3d 421, 423 (6th Cir. 1997) (*Feres* applied to suit by widow alleging Army failure to supervise her husband caused his suicide); Becker v. Pena, 1997 WL 90570, at *1 (9th Cir. Feb. 28, 1997) (*Feres* applied to suit against individual officers; "[h]er allegation that the defendants negligently failed to supervise the harassers 'goes directly to the "management" of the military; it calls into question basic choices about the discipline, supervision, and control of a service [member].'" (citing *Shearer*, 473 U.S. at 58 (1985)).

81. *Shearer*, 473 U.S. at 52.

82. *E.g.*, Smith v. United States, 196 F.3d 774, 776 (7th Cir. 1999) (sexual assault by drill sergeant); Stephenson v. Stone, 21 F.3d 159, 163 (7th Cir. 1994) (suit by personal representative and survivors of service member shot to death by sergeant with whom he had engaged in homosexual acts); McAllister v. United States, 942 F.2d 1473, 1477 (9th Cir. 1991) (suit by estate of officer stabbed to death by enlisted man who was being treated at base hospital for psychiatric problems); Dozler v. United States, 869 F.2d 1165, 1166 (8th Cir. 1989) (suit by personal representative of Army sergeant murdered by a another servicemember for money); Satterfield v. United States, 788 F.2d 395, 397 (6th Cir. 1986) (suit by administratrix of estate of Army private beaten to death by other members of his unit).

CHAPTER 4

Statutory Bars to FTCA Liability

Congress's authority to waive sovereign immunity for suits in tort includes the power to limit that waiver.[1] When it enacted the FTCA Congress included explicit exceptions for several categories of claims from the statute's general waiver of sovereign immunity.[2] If an FTCA exception applies the claim is barred.[3] Congress has enacted other laws that explicitly bar suit[4] or have been interpreted to bar claims that might otherwise fall within the FTCA's waiver of sovereign immunity.[5]

A. Exceptions in the Text of the FTCA

The first exception included in the FTCA is the due care exception of § 2680(a). It applies to "[a]ny claim based upon an act or omission of an employee of the Government, exercising due care, in the execution of a statute or regulation, whether or not such statute or

---

1. *See* United States v. Kubrick, 444 U.S. 111, 117–18 (1979) (stating that courts should not extend the waiver of sovereign immunity beyond that which Congress intended); *see also* LM *ex rel* KM v. United States, 344 F.3d 695, 698 (7th Cir. 2003) (explaining that the FTCA creates a broad waiver of sovereign immunity, but it is limited by the statutory exceptions).

2. These exceptions are codified at 28 U.S.C. § 2680(a)–(n) (2012) ("The provisions of this chapter and section 1346 (b) of this title shall not apply to—[listed claims].").

3. *See* Dolan v. U.S. Postal Serv., 546 U.S. 481, 485 (2006) ("The FTCA qualifies its waiver of sovereign immunity for certain categories of claims (13 in all). If one of the exceptions applies, the bar of sovereign immunity remains."); Dalehite v. United States, 346 U.S. 15, 32 (1953) ("One only need read § 2680 in its entirety to conclude that Congress exercised care to protect the Government from claims, however negligently caused, that affected the governmental functions.").

4. *See infra* Chapter 4.B.

5. *See infra* Chapter 4.C.

regulation be valid . . . ."[6] This provision prohibits "tests by tort action of the legality of statutes and regulations."[7] It applies when (1) a "federal statute, regulation, or policy specifically prescribes a course of action for an employee to follow" and (2) the employee uses "due care" in executing the statute or regulation.[8] In practice, it blocks tort suits that question a government action, taken with due care, that is authorized by a statute or regulation.[9] Accordingly, the due care exception bars FTCA suits such as those challenging an agency's interpretation of benefits available under its regulations[10] or its decision to release documents under the Freedom of Information Act.[11]

A second exception contained in § 2680(a), prohibits "[a]ny claim . . . based upon the exercise or performance or the failure to

---

6. 28 U.S.C. § 2680(a).

7. *Dalehite*, 346 U.S. at 33. The Court explained:

> It was not "intended that the constitutionality of legislation, the legality of regulations, or the propriety of a discretionary administrative act, should be tested through the medium of a damage suit for tort. The same holds true of other administrative action not of a regulatory nature, such as the expenditure of Federal funds, the execution of a Federal project and the like."

Id. at 27 (quoting Statement by Ass't Att'y Gen. Francis M. Shea at Hearings on H.R. 5373 and H.R. 6463 Before the House Comm. on the Judiciary, 77th Cong., 2d Sess. 6, 25, 33 (1942)).

8. Crumpton v. Stone, 59 F.3d 1400, 1403 (D.C. Cir. 1995) (barring suit by widow of military officer who alleged Army negligently released information about her and her family pursuant to FOIA request) (citing United States v. Gaubert, 499 U.S. 315, 322 (1991)).

9. *See, e.g.*, Welch v. United States, 409 F.3d 646, 652 (4th Cir. 2005) (barring suit by immigrant held in custody for 422 days under statute later declared unconstitutional as applied to him); Buchanan v. United States, 915 F.2d 969, 971 (5th Cir. 1990) (barring suit by prisoner noting that even if prison officials exercised due care, the claim would still be subject to the discretionary function exception); Lively v. United States, 870 F.2d 296, 298 (5th Cir. 1989) (barring claim by dockworkers for asbestos exposure; "[t]he first clause [of FTCA], excepting claims based on the execution of a statute or regulation, requires for its application that the actor have exercised due care. The second clause, excepting claims based on the performance of a discretionary function, has no such requirement."); *see also* LESTER S. JAYSON & ROBERT C. LONGSTRETH, HANDLING FEDERAL TORT CLAIMS § 12.03 (2018).

10. *See* Baie v. Secretary of Defense, 784 F.2d 1375, 1376 (9th Cir. 1986) ("We also agree with the district court that whether the Assistant Secretary's administrative interpretation of CHAMPUS excluding penile implants from the statute as 'prosthetic devices' was arbitrary or contrary to law may not be tested in an action under the FTCA.").

11. *See Crumpton*, 59 F.3d at 1403.

exercise or perform a discretionary function or duty on the part of a federal agency or an employee of the Government, whether or not the discretion involved be abused."[12] This is the discretionary function exception, often considered the most important FTCA exception.[13] The discretion protected by the exception, the discretion to exercise judgment, has roots deep in American jurisprudence:

> The "discretion" protected by the section is not that of the judge—a power to decide within the limits of positive rules of law subject to judicial review. It is the discretion of the executive or the administrator to act according to one's judgment of the best course, a concept of substantial historical ancestry in American law.[14]

As the Supreme Court explained in *Gaubert*, two elements must be met under the discretionary function exception.[15] First, a government action must "'involv[e] an element of judgment or choice.'"[16] There can be no judgment or choice if a "'federal statute, regulation or policy specifically prescribes a course of action for an employee to follow.'"[17] Second, the required judgment must involve social, economic, or political policy, the sort of judgments the exception was

---

12. 28 U.S.C. §2680(a).

13. *See* Gregory C. Sisk, *The Inevitability of Federal Sovereign Immunity*, 55 VILL. L. REV. 899, 919 (2010) (arguing discretionary function immunity properly preserves separation of powers); Vicki C. Jackson, *Suing the Federal Government: Sovereignty, Immunity, and Judicial Independence*, 35 GEO. WASH. INT'L L. REV. 521 (2003) ("Of [the FTCA exceptions], the most important is the 'discretionary function' exception.").

14. Dalehite v. United States, 346 U.S. 15, 34 (1953) (citing Perkins v. Lukens Steel Co., 310 U.S. 113, 131 (1940); *see also* Louisiana v. McAdoo, 234 U.S. 627, 633 (1914); Alzua v. Johnson, 231 U.S. 106, 111 (1913); Spalding v. Vilas, 161 U.S. 483, 498 (1896); Marbury v. Madison, 5 U.S. (1 Cranch) 137, 170 (1803)).

15. Gaubert v. United States, 499 U.S. 315, 322–23.

16. *Id.* at 322 (quoting Berkovitz v. United States, 486 U.S. 531, 536 (1988)).

17. *Id.*

intended to protect.[18] This test is met if the actions taken are "susceptible to policy analysis," regardless of whether the employee consciously made a policy determination.[19] Nor does it matter whether the decision was made at the planning or operational level.[20] "It is the nature of the conduct, rather than the status of the actor, that governs whether the discretionary function exception applies . . . ."[21] As a consequence, a detailed factual record is not required: *Gaubert* was resolved on a motion to dismiss.[22] Because the exception, by its terms, is applicable "whether or not the discretion involved be abused,"[23] when its elements are met it bars claims arising from flawed policies or negligent conduct.[24]

The discretionary function exception applies to a broad range of decisions. The Supreme Court has held it bars suits alleging that the fire that destroyed Texas City was the result of negligence in the

---

18. *Id.* at 322–23. The Court explained:

> Furthermore, even "assuming the challenged conduct involves an element of judgment," it remains to be decided "whether that judgment is of the kind that the discretionary function exception was designed to shield." [*Berkovitz*, 486 U.S. at 536]. See *Varig Airlines*, 467 U.S., at 813. Because the purpose of the exception is to "prevent judicial 'second-guessing' of legislative and administrative decisions grounded in social, economic, and political policy through the medium of an action in tort," *id.*, at 814, when properly construed, the exception "protects only governmental actions and decisions based on considerations of public policy." Berkovitz, *supra*, at 537.

> *Id.*

19. *Gaubert*, 499 U.S. at 324–25:

> For a complaint to survive a motion to dismiss, it must allege facts which would support a finding that the challenged actions are not the kind of conduct that can be said to be grounded in the policy of the regulatory regime. The focus of the inquiry is not on the agent's subjective intent in exercising the discretion conferred by statute or regulation, but on the nature of the actions taken and on whether they are susceptible to policy analysis.

20. *Id.* at 325 ("A discretionary act is one that involves choice or judgment; there is nothing in that description that refers exclusively to policymaking or planning functions.").

21. *Id.* at 322 (quoting United States v. Varig Airlines, 467 U.S. 797, 813 (1984)).

22. *Id.* at 320.

23. 28 U.S.C. § 2680(a).

24. *See* Dalehite v. United States, 346 U.S. 15, 22–23, 43 (1953); Domme v. United States, 61 F.3d 787, 789 (10th Cir. 1995) (rejecting argument that the exception "does not apply to 'mandatory common law duties'" to supervise contractor operating government owned national laboratories).

program to send fertilizer to post–World War II Europe,[25] that airplanes crashed because the Federal Aviation Administration delegated safety inspections,[26] and that a bank failed because of poor "day-to-day" decisions made by government-appointed bank managers.[27] On the other hand, the Court held the exception did not apply to a suit alleging that polio vaccine was licensed for release to the public in contravention of mandatory agency regulations that set specific scientific standards for that licensing.[28]

The exception bars suits arising from broad decisions of nation-wide import such as President Carter's determination to cancel wheat sales in retaliation for the Soviet Union's invasion of Afghanistan,[29] President Reagan's decision to order missile strikes on Tripoli and Benghazi in response to acts of terrorism instigated by the Libyan government,[30] and the FDA Commissioner's order prohibiting importation of Chilean grapes even though that order was based on allegedly negligent laboratory work.[31] It also bars claims for smaller, everyday events such as falling trees (if forestry officials

---

25. *Dalehite*, 346 U.S. at 22–23, 43. The Supreme Court included in the Appendix to its decision the district court's findings of numerous "blunders, mistakes, and acts of negligence, both of omission and commission, on the part of Defendant" in the fertilizer program. *Id.* at 45–46. The district court found negligence in the decisions to begin the program, continue the program, to use a material to coat the fertilizer, to use paper bags for shipping, to pack the fertilizer so it did not cool, to not label it as an explosive, and to not notify the carriers, the city or the state of its dangers. *Id.* at 45–47.

26. *Varig Airlines*, 467 U.S. at 820.

27. *Gaubert*, 499 U.S. at 319–20:

> [Government-substituted bank officers] recommended the hiring of a certain consultant to advise IASA on operational and financial matters; they advised IASA concerning whether, when, and how its subsidiaries should be placed into bankruptcy; they mediated salary disputes; they reviewed the draft of a complaint to be used in litigation; they urged IASA to convert from state to federal charter; and they actively intervened when the Texas Savings and Loan Department attempted to install a supervisory agent at IASA.

28. Berkovitz v. United States, 486 U.S. 531 at 546–47 (1988).

29. Galloway Farms, Inc. v. United States, 834 F.2d 998, 1004 (Fed. Cir. 1987).

30. Saltany v. Reagan, 886 F.2d 438 (D.C. Cir. 1989) (per curiam), *aff'g in relevant part and rev'g in part*, 702 F. Supp. 319 (D.D.C. 1988), *cert. denied*, 495 U.S. 932 (1990), *op. after remand, reh'g denied sub nom.* Saltany v. Bush, 960 F.2d 1060 (D.C. Cir.), *cert. denied sub nom.* Clark v. Thatcher, 506 U.S. 956 (1992).

31. Fisher Bros. Sales, Inc. v. United States, 46 F.3d 279, 285–86 (3d Cir. 1995) (alleging that laboratory negligently concluded that sample grapes contained poison).

have discretion to determine what inspections to conduct),[32] the sale of used motor vehicles "as-is" (if the terms of sale involve policy considerations),[33] or failing to manage or destroy dangerous wildlife in national parks.[34]

The next exception, § 2680(b), bars suit for "any claim arising out of the loss, miscarriage, or negligent transmission of letters or postal matter."[35] It applies only to claims relating to the transmittal of the mails. The postal exception bars suits for late deliveries,[36] lost items,[37] and stolen mail containing incredibly valuable works of art created by the sender.[38] The exception has also been applied to suits against the Postal Service for transmitting mail bombs.[39] The postal exception does not bar claims tangentially related to mail transmittal, such as leaving mail where it can cause a slip and fall,[40] negligently driving postal trucks,[41] or surreptitiously reading the mail.[42]

---

32. Autery v. United States, 992 F.2d 1523, 1528 (11th Cir. 1993) (barring suit where black locust fell on decedent's car while he drove through Great Smokey Mountain National Park).

33. Myslakowski v. United States, 806 F.2d 94, 98 (6th Cir. 1986) (barring suit for failure to warn arising from vehicle rollover where sale of used postal vehicles "as-is-where-is" "included, inferentially, no test driving, no mechanical inspection, no refurbishing or reconditioning, no express warranties, and certainly no warnings.").

34. Chadd v. United States, 794 F.3d 1104, 1113 (9th Cir. 2015) (alleging negligent failure to destroy dangerous mountain goat); Tippett v. United States, 108 F.3d 1194, 1199 (10th Cir. 1997) ("it is irrelevant whether Ranger Phillips directed plaintiffs into danger . . . . Even if discretion is exercised negligently, the exception [bars suit]. The relevant inquiry is whether Ranger Phillips was exercising discretion grounded in public policy when he directed plaintiffs around the moose." (citing United States v. Domme, 61 F.3d 787, 789 (10th Cir. 1995)).

35. 28 U.S.C. § 2680(b).

36. See Rider v. U.S. Postal Serv., 862 F.2d 239, 242 (9th Cir. 1988) (political mail delivered too late to be used).

37. See Georgacarakos v. United States, 420 F.3d 1185, 1186 (10th Cir. 2005) (barring suit by prisoner for loss of sixteen of twenty-three books mailed together in a box).

38. In Anderson v. U.S. Postal Serv., 761 F.2d 527, 528 (9th Cir. 1985), plaintiff, a composer, mailed some of his original compositions to himself and insured them for $100. When his package was stolen he brought suit for $800,000. Id. The court affirmed dismissal based on the postal exception. Id.

39. See Gager v. United States, 149 F.3d 918, 920–22 (9th Cir. 1998) (mail bomb delivered to home of Nevada Highway Patrol trooper).

40. Dolan v. U.S. Postal Serv., 546 U.S. 481, 486 (2006).

41. See generally id. at 487–88.

42. Cruikshank v. United States, 431 F. Supp. 1355, 1360 (D. Haw. 1977).

The exception set forth at § 2680(c), blocks "claim[s] arising in respect of the assessment or collection of any tax or customs duty, or the detention of . . . property by any . . . law enforcement officer . . . ."[43] The first clause bars tort suits pertaining to taxes, such as those alleging that a tax-sale was mishandled,[44] bank and retirement accounts were improperly attached,[45] or tax refunds were not properly paid.[46] The second clause bars suit for detention of goods, whether the claim is for a wrongful detention[47] or for loss or damage

---

43. The exception states:

> (c) Any claim arising in respect of the assessment or collection of any tax or customs duty, or the detention of any goods, merchandise, or other property by any officer of customs or excise or any other law enforcement officer, except that the provisions of this chapter [28 U.S.C. §§ 2671 et seq.] and section 1346(b) of this title apply to any claim based on injury or loss of goods, merchandise, or other property, while in the possession of any officer of customs or excise or any other law enforcement officer, if—
>
> (1) the property was seized for the purpose of forfeiture under any provision of Federal law providing for the forfeiture of property other than as a sentence imposed upon conviction of a criminal offense;
>
> (2) the interest of the claimant was not forfeited;
>
> (3) the interest of the claimant was not remitted or mitigated (if the property was subject to forfeiture); and
>
> (4) the claimant was not convicted of a crime for which the interest of the claimant in the property was subject to forfeiture under a Federal criminal forfeiture law.[.]

28 U.S.C. § 2680(c).
44. *See* Green v. United States, 434 F. Supp. 2d 1116, 1127–28 (D. Utah 2006).
45. *See* Weiner v. Internal Revenue Service, 986 F.2d 12, 12–13 (2d Cir. 1993).
46. *See* Aetna Cas. & Sur. Co. v. United States, 71 F.3d 475, 477–78 (2d Cir. 1995).
47. *See* United States v. $149,345 U.S. Currency, 747 F.2d 1278, 1283 (9th Cir. 1984). The court explained:

> The [claim] also falls outside the Federal Tort Claims Act because the alleged injury arises from the detention of the money itself and the propriety of the detention is at issue. 28 U.S.C. § 2680(c) excludes from [the FTCA] claims for detention of goods or merchandise by law enforcement officers . . . . The apparent intent of section 2680(c) is to limit governmental liability for improper seizures and to restrict claimants to the statutory procedures of the forfeiture laws. . . . These aims are just as important for seizures of currency as for merchandise.

Id. (internal citations omitted).

to detained goods.[48] The detention of goods clause applies whenever any law enforcement officer (not just those enforcing customs or excise laws) holds, ships, or stores detained goods.[49]

The three subsequent exceptions are straightforward and rarely litigated. Section 2680(d) applies to claims that are cognizable under the Suits in Admiralty Act or the Public Vessels Act.[50] Section 2680(e) applies to claims arising from administration of the Trading with the Enemy Act.[51] Section 2680(f) addresses "Any claim for damages caused by the imposition or establishment of a quarantine by the United States."[52] Many of the cases that address the quarantine exception involve agriculture.[53]

The next provision,[54] § 2680(h), the intentional tort exception, retains sovereign immunity for claims arising from the eleven specific torts it names.[55] It bars claims for assault or battery by federal

---

48. Kosak v. United States, 465 U.S. 848, 862 (1984) ("The Tort Claims Act does not cover suits alleging that customs officials injured property that had been detained by the Customs Service.").

49. *See* Ali v. Fed. Bureau of Prisons, 552 U.S. 214, 220–21 (2008) (barring suit by federal prisoner who alleged his property was lost during transfer to another prison).

50. It bars "[a]ny claim for which a remedy is provided by sections 741-52, 781–790 of Title 46, relating to claims or suits in admiralty against the United States." 28 U.S.C. § 2680(d). *See* Kelly v. United States, 531 F.2d 1144, 1149 (2d Cir. 1976) (barring claim alleging negligent Coast Guard failure to rescue when nineteen-foot sailboat capsized on Lake Ontario; "decedent's claim should have been brought under the Suits in Admiralty Act . . . and it cannot be maintained under 28 U.S.C. § 1346(b) because of the express prohibition of 28 U.S.C. § 2680(d).").

51. It bars "[a]ny claim arising out of an act or omission of any employee of the Government in administering the provisions of sections 1-31 of Title 50, Appendix." 28 U.S.C. § 2680(e); *see* Price v. United States, 69 F.3d 46, 52 (5th Cir. 1995) (barring claim for value of watercolors painted by Hitler and Nazi photographs seized under the Trading with the Enemy Act).

52. 2. 8 U.S.C. § 2680(f).

53. *See, e.g.*, Rey v. United States, 484 F.2d 45, 46 (5th Cir. 1973) (barring suit where hogs died from cholera vaccine after other hogs were quarantined with cholera); Saxton v. United States, 456 F.2d 1105, 1106 (8th Cir. 1972) (barring claim that alleged "emotional injury from the quarantining of samples taken from the [plaintiffs'] cattle").

54. Section 2680(g) was repealed. Sept. 26, 1950, c. 1049, § 13(5), 64 Stat. 1043.

55. It bars "[a]ny claim arising out of assault, battery, false imprisonment, false arrest, malicious prosecution, abuse of process, libel, slander, misrepresentation, deceit, or interference with contract rights . . . ." 28 U.S.C. § 2680(h).

employees and applies whether harm was intended,[56] a joke ran afoul,[57] or plaintiff characterizes the act as negligent.[58] The assault and battery exception does not apply to claims for medical malpractice.[59] Nor does it apply if acts of other government employees give rise to a separate cause of action. In *Sheridan v. United States,* where a patient at Bethesda Naval Hospital fired a gun at passing motorists, the Supreme Court explained that "the negligence of other Government employees who allowed a foreseeable assault and battery to occur may furnish a basis for Government liability . . . ."[60]

Section 2680(h) also bars claims for false imprisonment, false arrest, malicious prosecution, and abuse of process. Prior to 1974, these exceptions, and the assault and battery exception, were important in suits alleging wrongdoing by federal law enforcement officials.[61] In 1974, Congress determined that the FTCA should provide a remedy for such torts.[62] Accordingly, it amended § 2680(h) by adding

---

56. *See* Turner v. United States, 595 F. Supp. 708, 709 (W.D. La. 1984) (barring suit where military recruiter "deceived four . . . adult women, into believing that in order to join the [National] Guard, they had to submit to complete physical examinations conducted on the spot by him as the recruiter").

57. *See* Lambertson v. United States, 528 F.2d 441, 442 (2d Cir. 1976) (barring suit where meat inspector "pulled plaintiff's wool stocking hat over his eyes and, climbing on his back, began to ride him piggyback" causing his face to strike meat hooks).

58. *See* United States v. Faneca, 332 F.2d 872, 875 (5th Cir. 1964) (barring suit for injuries from tear gas used by federal officials confronting hostile crowd when James Meredith entered the University of Mississippi; "[n]or can plaintiff recover under the Tort Claims Act for the 'negligent' firing on him by the group of marshals and Border Patrolmen.").

59. *See* Keir v. United States, 853 F.2d 398, 410–11 (6th Cir. 1988). The Gonzalez Act, 10 U.S.C. § 1089, makes the FTCA the exclusive remedy available for malpractice by armed forces medical personnel. In *Levin v. United States,* 568 U.S. 503, 518 (2013), the Supreme Court held that the Gonzalez Act "abrogates the FTCA's intentional tort exception and therefore permits suit[s] against the United States alleging medical battery by a [military] doctor acting within the scope of his employment." (citing 10 U.S.C. § 1089(e)).

60. Sheridan v. United States, 487 U.S. 392, 401 (1988), *dismissed on remand* 969 F.2d 72, 74 (4th Cir. 1992) (finding no actionable duty under Maryland law), *aff'g* 773 F. Supp. 786 (D. Md. 1991).

61. *See, e.g.,* Swanson v. Willis, 220 F.2d 440, 440 (9th Cir. 1955) (per curiam) (affirming dismissal of suit against Deputy U.S. Marshall that alleged false arrest and battery in the course of an arrest); Jones v. Fed. Bureau of Investigation, 139 F. Supp. 38, 40–41 (D. Md. 1956) (dismissing under § 2680(h) complaint that alleged FBI agents threatened plaintiff's "sick wife and three little children for a period of 20 to 30 minutes," falsely imprisoned them and plaintiff in an apartment, carried plaintiff away, and stole his property).

62. *See* S. Rep. 93-588, S. Rep. No. 588, 93rd Cong., 2d Sess. 1974, 1974 U.S.C.C.A.N. 2789 at 2791.

a proviso that voids the FTCA exceptions for assault, battery, false imprisonment, false arrest, malicious prosecution, and abuse of process for acts of federal law enforcement officers. The Senate Report stated:

> The effect of this provision is to deprive the Federal Government of the defense of sovereign immunity in cases in which Federal law enforcement agents, acting within the scope of their employment, or under color of Federal law, commit any of the following torts: assault, battery, false imprisonment, false arrest, malicious prosecution, or abuse of process. Thus, after the date of enactment of this measure, innocent individuals who are subjected to raids of the type conducted in Collinsville, Illinois, will have a cause of action against the individual Federal agents and the Federal Government.[63]

The law enforcement proviso is an exception to the § 2680(h) exception to the FTCA's general waiver of sovereign immunity. In *Millbrook v. United States*, the Supreme Court held that the proviso "extends to acts or omissions of law enforcement officers that arise within the scope of their employment, regardless of whether the officers are engaged in investigative or law enforcement activity, or are executing a search, seizing evidence, or making an arrest."[64] The proviso does not apply to prosecutors and other federal employees who are not law enforcement officers, leaving the § 2680(h) bar in place

---

63. Pub. L. No. 93-253, 88 Stat. 50 (Mar. 16, 1974) added the following language to 2680(h):

> Provided, That, with regard to acts or omissions of investigative or law enforcement officers of the United States Government, the provisions of this chapter and section 1346 (b) of this title shall apply to any claim arising, on or after the date of the enactment of this proviso, out of assault, battery, false imprisonment, false arrest, abuse of process, or malicious prosecution. For the purpose of this subsection, "investigative or law enforcement officer" means any officer of the United States who is empowered by law to execute searches, to seize evidence, or to make arrests for violations of Federal law.

64. Millbrook v. United States, 569 U.S. 50, 57 (2013) (permitting suit that alleged sexual and verbal harassment by Bureau of Prisons correctional officers).

as to their acts of assault, battery, false imprisonment, false arrest, or malicious prosecution.[65]

Section 2680(h) also bars claims for libel or slander, for misrepresentation or deceit, and for interference with contract rights. The libel and slander exception bars traditional claims for libel and slander[66] and other claims for which defamation is a necessary element.[67] It does not bar claims for invasion of privacy except those based on false statements.[68]

The misrepresentation exception applies when a plaintiff's injury arises from its reliance on information communicated by the government. Two Supreme Court cases delineate its scope. First, in *United States v. Neustadt*,[69] the purchaser of a house that had been appraised

---

65. *See, e.g.*, Gen. Dynamics Corp. v. United States, 139 F.3d 1280, 1286 (9th Cir. 1998) (holding prosecutors are not law enforcement officers, "[w]here, as here, the harm actually flows from the prosecutor's exercise of discretion, an attempt to recharacterize the action as something else must fail"); Wilson v. United States, 959 F.2d 12, 14 (2d Cir. 1992) (holding parole officers are not law enforcement officers); Ames v. United States, 600 F.2d 183, 185 n.3 (8th Cir. 1979) (reading the proviso as not applicable to United States Attorney); Solomon v. United States, 559 F.2d 309, 310 (5th Cir. 1977) (holding Post Exchange security employees are not law enforcement officers).

66. *See* Cooper v. Am. Auto. Ins. Co., 978 F.2d 602, 613 (10th Cir. 1992) (barring claim alleging that federal "employees negligently brought false information to the attention of third parties"); Council on Am. Islamic Relations, Inc. v. Ballenger, 366 F. Supp. 2d 28, 30, 32 (D.D.C. 2005) (barring suit for Congressman's statement, given in interview about his marital problems, that characterized his neighbor "as the 'fund-raising arm for Hezbullah'").

67. *See* Art Metal-USA, Inc. v. United States, 753 F.2d 1151, 1156 (D.C. Cir. 1985) (rejecting argument that claim for injurious falsehood is not encompassed by the libel and slander exception; "Art Metal's argument . . . is based on an illusory distinction between its interest in its reputation (which would be vindicated by a defamation action showing lost profits) and its pecuniary interest in its products (which would be vindicated by an injurious falsehood action requiring pecuniary harm).").

68. *Compare* Birnbaum v. United States, 588 F.2d 319, 328 (2d Cir. 1978) (holding that § 2680(h) did not bar invasion of privacy claim where CIA had opened and read plaintiff's mail; "the torts of trespass and invasion of privacy do not fall within the exception of § 2680(h)."), *with* Metz v. United States, 788 F.2d 1528, 1535 (11th Cir. 1986):

> the government officials' allegedly slanderous statements are essential to Mr. Metz's action for false light privacy and Ingrid Metz's claim for intentional infliction of emotional distress. See Block v. Neal, 460 U.S. at 297–99. There is no other governmental action upon which these claims could rest. These claims, therefore, "arise out of" slander for the purposes of § 2680(h) and are not actionable under the FTCA.

69. 366 U.S. 696 (1961).

by the Federal Housing Administration alleged that in reliance on the agency's negligent inspection and appraisal he had paid a price above the fair market value.[70] The Court held that regardless of whether the FHA was negligent or owed plaintiff a "'specific duty' to obtain and communicate information carefully," the misrepresentation exception barred his claim because plaintiff's injuries resulted from his reliance on the FHA's statement.[71]

In the second case, *Block v. Neal*, the plaintiff had obtained a loan from the FHA for a prefabricated house.[72] After plaintiff moved into the house, she discovered defects she attributed to FHA's negligence in supervising its construction.[73] The FHA argued that plaintiff's claim was one of "misrepresentation" and, therefore, barred by § 2680(h).[74] The Court rejected the argument, noting "the Government's misstatements are not essential to plaintiff's negligence claim."[75] It held that the misrepresentation exception "does not bar negligence actions which focus not on the Government's failure to use due care in communicating information, but rather on the Government's breach of a different duty."[76]

---

70. *Id.* at 700–01.

71. *Id.* at 710–11.

72. 460 U.S. 289, 291 (1983).

73. *Id.* at 290.

74. *Id.* at 296.

75. *Id.* at 297.

76. *Id.* In *Block*, the Court reaffirmed its *Neustadt* holding: "Neustadt alleged no injury that he would have suffered independently of his reliance on the erroneous appraisal. Because the alleged conduct that was the basis of his negligence claim was in essence a negligent misrepresentation, Neustadt's action was barred under the 'misrepresentation' exception." *Id.* at 296–97.

The exception applies whether the misrepresentation is inten-tional[77] or negligent.[78] It bars suit for both commercial losses[79] and personal injuries.[80] Because it is inapplicable when the government owes a separate duty, the exception does not bar suits arising from medical malpractice[81] or faulty navigational aids.[82]

The exception for "interference with contract rights"[83] has been applied to claims of interference with employment,[84] debarment from government contracts,[85] and seizure of assets.[86] It applies whether the

---

77. *See* Frigard v. United States, 862 F.2d 201, 202 (9th Cir. 1988) (barring suit by swindled investors where "[t]he gravamen of their complaint alleged that the CIA used BBRDW [an investment company] as a cover for its operations; wrongfully permitted . . . the firm president, to defraud investors; and misrepresented that BBRDW was a legitimate company"); Redmond v. United States, 518 F.2d 811, 812 (7th Cir. 1975) (barring claims that agents and operatives of the government permitted plaintiff to be defrauded by a "securities dealer" described as a "highly competent confidence man working with govern-ment agents to recover a stolen U.S. Treasury bond").

78. *See* United States v. Neustadt, 366 U.S. 696, 702 (1961) ("§ 2680(h) comprehends claims arising out of negligent, as well as willful, misrepresentation.").

79. *See* Reamer v. United States, 459 F.2d 709, 710 (4th Cir. 1972) (barring suit for misrepresentation that law student could defer active duty until completion of semester if he enlisted, resulting in monetary loss when he was ordered to active duty).

80. *See* Schneider v. United States, 936 F.2d 956, 962 (7th Cir. 1991) (barring suit for personal injury caused by construction defects in manufactured homes; "the govern-ment's communication of its approval of Tri State's plans created the assurance that the plaintiffs relied on to their detriment."); Bergquist v. United States, 849 F. Supp. 1221, 1231 (N.D. Ill. 1994) (barring claim that the National Weather Service negligently issued tornado warnings); Vaughn v. United States, 259 F. Supp. 286, 287–88 (N.D. Miss. 1966) (barring claim where construction crew relied on government map and unexpectedly struck gas pipeline).

81. *See* Beech v. United States, 345 F.2d 872, 874 (5th Cir. 1965); Phillips v. United States, 508 F. Supp. 544, 548 (D.S.C. 1981).

82. *See* Ingham v. Eastern Air Lines, Inc., 373 F.2d 227, 239 (2d Cir. 1967) (allowing suit where air traffic controllers failed to provide accurate weather information).

83. The Restatement (Second) of Torts, § 766 (1977) identifies an action for "'inducing breach of contract or refusal to deal" as an act by someone not privileged to do so, that "induces or otherwise purposely causes a third person not to (a) perform a contract with another, or (b) enter into or continue a business relation with another, is liable to the other for the harm caused thereby."

84. *See* Moessmer v. United States, 760 F.2d 236, 237 (8th Cir. 1985) (barring claim that CIA pressured private firm to not hire former agency employee; "[w]e hold that Moess-mer's claim for interference with prospective economic advantage is the equivalent of a claim for interference with contract rights, and thus falls within the section 2680(h) exemption.").

85. *See* Art Metal-USA, Inc. v. United States, 753 F.2d 1151, 1155 (D.C. Cir. 1985).

86. *See* United States v. Mullins, 228 F. Supp. 748, 750 (W.D. Va. 1964).

interference is caused by government conspiracy[87] or simple bureau-cratic delay.[88]

There are limits on the scope of §2680(h). In addition to the law enforcement proviso,[89] it does not apply to claims arising from "the provision of legal assistance" by members of a legal staff of the Department of Defense or the Coast Guard.[90] Nor does it apply to intentional torts it does not list such as trespass,[91] conversion,[92] intentional infliction of emotional distress,[93] or invasion of privacy[94] so long as none of the excepted torts is a necessary part of the claim.[95] The Supreme Court, however, has rejected attempts to avoid the effect of the § 2680 exceptions by artful pleading, suggesting that the courts must "look beyond the literal meaning of the language to ascertain the real cause of complaint."[96]

---

87. *See* Daisley v. Riggs Bank, N.A., 372 F. Supp. 2d 61, 64 (D.D.C. 2005) (barring claim that Treasury official and bank officer "conspired to orchestrate [plaintiff's] termination").

88. *See* Shapiro v. United States, 566 F. Supp. 886, 888 (E.D. Pa. 1983) (barring claim of former State Department attorney who "averred that the Government's negligence in providing a letter concerning his conflict of interest situation delayed the beginning of his association with [a law firm].").

89. *See supra* notes 62–63 and accompanying text.

90. *See* 10 U.S.C. § 1054(e).

91. *See* Ira S. Bushey & Sons, Inc. v. United States, 276 F. Supp. 518, 526 (E.D.N.Y. 1967), *aff'd*, 398 F.2d 167 (2d Cir. 1968) (intoxicated seaman opened floodgate valves on floating drydock).

92. Preston v. United States, 596 F.2d 232, 239–40 (7th Cir. 1979) (Commodity Credit Corporation kept farmers' share of proceeds of grain sold from bankrupt warehouse).

93. Truman v. United States, 26 F.3d 592, 597 (5th Cir. 1994) (sexual harassment not involving assault or battery); Gross v. United States, 676 F.2d 295, 298 (8th Cir. 1982) (farmer unfairly excluded from participating in Department of Agriculture feed grain program); Cruikshank v. United States, 431 F. Supp. 1355, 1360 (D. Haw. 1977) (opening plaintiff's mail).

94. Birnbaum v. United States, 588 F.2d 319, 328 (2d Cir. 1978) (allowing invasion of privacy claim where CIA opened and read plaintiff's mail; "the torts of trespass and invasion of privacy do not fall within the exception of §2680(h).").

95. *See, e.g.*, Art Metal-USA, Inc. v. United States, 753 F.2d 1151, 1156 (D.C. Cir. 1985) (rejecting argument that claim for injurious falsehood is not encompassed by the libel and slander exception).

96. United States v. Neustadt, 366 U.S. 696, 703 (1961); United States v. Shearer, 473 U.S. 52, 55 (1985) (plurality opinion) ("No semantical recasting of events can alter the fact that the battery was the immediate cause of [the injury] and consequently, the basis of respondent's claim.").

Section 2680(i) applies to "[a]ny claim for damages caused by the fiscal operations of the Treasury or by the regulation of the monetary system."[97] It rarely comes up.[98]

The combatant activity exception of § 2680(j) bars all claims arising from "combatant activities."[99] The term includes "not only physical violence, but activities both necessary to and in direct connection with actual hostilities."[100] The exception applies regardless of whether there is a formal declaration of war.[101] In *Koohi v. United States*, the Ninth Circuit applied the combatant activities exception to bar suit when a U.S. warship mistakenly shot down an Iranian civilian aircraft, noting that the exception is intended "to ensure that the government will not be liable for negligent conduct by our armed forces in times of combat."[102]

The foreign tort exception of §2680(k) bars "claim[s] arising in a foreign country." In its 2004 *Sosa v. Alvarez-Machain* opinion, the Supreme Court held that the "foreign country exception bars all claims based on any injury suffered in a foreign country, regardless of where the tortious act or omission occurred."[103] In doing so it rejected a prior line of cases that allowed suit to proceed if plaintiffs alleged that a tort in the United States caused injury in a foreign land.[104] The exception applies whenever injury is suffered in foreign

---

97. 28 U.S.C. § 2680(i).

98. *See* Forrester v. U.S. Gov't, 443 F. Supp. 115, 118 (S.D.N.Y. 1977) (noting that the FTCA did not waive sovereign immunity for claims "seeking damages caused by the fiscal operations of the Treasury or by the regulation of the monetary system").

99. It applies to "claim[s] arising out of the combatant activities of the military or naval forces, or Coast Guard, during time of war." 28 U.S.C. § 2680(j).

100. *See* Koohi v. United States, 976 F.2d 1328, 1333 (9th Cir. 1992) (quoting Johnson v. United States, 170 F.2d 767, 770 (9th Cir. 1948) (holding exception did not bar suit for pollution of U.S. coastal waters by warships after conclusion of World War II)).

101. *See* Clark v. United States, 974 F. Supp. 895, 898 (E.D. Tex. 1996) (Operation Desert Storm), *aff'd without published opinion*, 116 F.3d 476 (5th Cir. 1997) (unpublished table decision); *Koohi*, 976 F.2d at 1334 (1988 tanker war with Iran); Rotko v. Abrams, 338 F. Supp. 46, 47 (D. Conn. 1971) (Vietnam War), *aff'd on basis of dist. ct. opinion*, 455 F.2d 992 (2d Cir. 1972).

102. *Koohi*, 976 F.2d at 1334 ("it simply does not matter for purposes of the 'time of war' exception whether the military makes or executes its decisions carefully or negligently, properly or improperly. It is the nature of the act and not the manner of its performance that counts.").

103. Sosa v. Alvarez-Machain, 542 U.S. 692, 712 (2004) (alleging that DEA improperly procured the kidnapping of plaintiff so that he could be tried in the United States for complicity in the torture and murder in Mexico of a DEA agent).

104. *See id.* at 709–12.

lands, including injuries that arise at U.S. embassies,[105] on U.S. military bases,[106] or in ungoverned regions.[107]

The three remaining exceptions are rarely litigated. They bar claims arising from the activities of "the Tennessee Valley Authority,"[108] "the Panama Canal Company,"[109] or "a Cooperative Bank, a Federal Land Bank or a Federal Intermediate Credit Bank."[110]

B. Statutes That Explicitly Bar Suit

A number of statutes preclude government liability under the FTCA for various kinds of claims. Some create their own comprehensive systems and explicitly prohibit any other judicial remedy. The Federal Employee's Compensation Act (FECA)[111] provides a comprehensive, workers' compensation–type remedy for federal employees killed or injured on the job that is exclusive[112] and bars any FTCA suit if a

---

105. *See* Meredith v. United States, 330 F.2d 9, 11 (9th Cir. 1964) (barring claim arising at U.S. embassy in Bangkok, Thailand; "[t]here is nothing in the Federal Tort Claims Act which indicates that it was intended to apply to personal or property damage sustained in our embassies and consulates abroad.").

106. *See* United States v. Spelar, 338 U.S. 217, 219 (1949) (barring claim arising at U.S. airfield in Newfoundland); Bird v. United States, 923 F. Supp. 338, 340 (D. Conn. 1996) (barring claim by wife of serviceman for medical malpractice at the United States Naval Facility, Guantanamo Bay, Cuba).

107. *See* Smith v. United States, 507 U.S. 197, 201–05 (1993) (barring claim that arose in Antarctica).

108. Section 2680(l) applies to "[a]ny claim arising from the activities of the Tennessee Valley Authority." 28 U.S.C. § 2680(l).

109. Section 2680(m) applies to "[a]ny claim arising from the activities of the Panama Canal Company." 28 U.S.C. § 2680(m).

110. Section 2680(n) applies to "[a]ny claim arising from the activities of a Federal land bank, a Federal intermediate credit bank, or a bank for cooperatives." 28 U.S.C. § 2680(n).

111. 5 U.S.C. § 8101 *et seq.*

112. 5 U.S.C. § 8116 (c):

> The liability of the United States or an instrumentality thereof under this subchapter [5 U.S.C. §§ 8101 et seq.] or any extension thereof with respect to the injury or death of an employee is exclusive and instead of all other liability of the United States or the instrumentality to the employee, his legal representative, spouse, dependents, next of kin, and any other person otherwise entitled to recover damages from the United States or the instrumentality because of the injury or death in a direct judicial proceeding, in a civil action, or in admiralty, or by an administrative or judicial proceeding under a workmen's compensation statute or under a Federal tort liability statute.

FECA remedy may be available.[113] The Longshore and Harbor Workers' Compensation Act also provides an exclusive, workers' compensation remedy for, *inter alia*, employees of nonappropriated fund instrumentalities.[114] Similarly, there are explicit provisions barring FTCA suits for the denial of Social Security,[115] Medicare,[116] and veterans' program benefits.[117]

Other statutes explicitly bar specific categories of claims. Perhaps the most important is the Flood Control Act of 1928, which provides, "No liability of any kind shall attach to or rest upon the United States for any damage from or by floods or flood waters at

---

113. Sw. Marine, Inc. v. Gizoni, 502 U.S. 81, 90 (1991) ("FECA contains an 'unambiguous and comprehensive' provision barring any judicial review of the Secretary of Labor's determination of FECA coverage. . . . Consequently, the courts have no jurisdiction over FTCA claims where the Secretary determines that FECA applies.") (internal citations omitted); Grijalva v. United States, 781 F.2d 472, 474 (5th Cir. 1986) (holding that plaintiff who received FECA benefits for injuries from auto accident "cannot now collaterally attack the Secretary's determination of coverage in this Tort Claims Act suit").

114. 5 U.S.C. § 8173 ("This liability is exclusive and instead of all other liability of the United States . . . in a civil action, or in admiralty, or by an administrative or judicial proceeding under a workmen's compensation statute or under a Federal tort liability statute.").

115. 42 U.S.C. § 405(h) ("Finality of Commissioner's decision. . . . No action against the United States, the Commissioner of Social Security, or any officer or employee thereof shall be brought under section 1331 or 1346 of title 28, United States Code [the FTCA], to recover on any claim arising under this title.").

116. The Medicare statue incorporates the § 405(h) rule from the Social Security Act 42 U.S.C. § 1395ii "application of certain provisions of title II [42 U.S.C. §§ 401 et seq.]" states:

> The provisions of sections 206 and 216(j), and of subsections (a), (d), (e), (h), (i), (j), (k), and (l) of section 205 [42 U.S.C. §§ 406, 416(j), and 405(a), (d), (e), (h), (i), (j), (k), and (l)], shall also apply with respect to this title [42 U.S.C. §§ 1395 et seq.] to the same extent as they are applicable with respect to title II [42 U.S.C. §§ 401 et seq.], except that, in applying such provisions with respect to this title, any reference therein to the Commissioner of Social Security or the Social Security Administration shall be considered a reference to the Secretary or the Department of Health and Human Services, respectively.

117. 38 U.S.C. § 511. Decisions of the Secretary; finality

> (a) The Secretary shall decide all questions of law and fact necessary to a decision by the Secretary under a law that affects the provision of benefits by the Secretary to veterans or the dependents or survivors of veterans. Subject to subsection (b), the decision of the Secretary as to any such question shall be final and conclusive and may not be reviewed by any other official or by any court, whether by an action in the nature of mandamus or otherwise.

any place . . . ."[118] The Supreme Court addressed the Flood Control Act twice in a five-year span. In *United States v. James* it held that the statute barred claims of recreational boaters who were injured or drowned when waters retained in flood control projects were released.[119] In *Central Green Co. v. United States*, the Supreme Court held that the Flood Control Act would not bar a claim that the design and construction of a multipurpose canal damaged an orchard unless floodwaters were involved in the injury.[120] The Court explained, "the text of the statute directs us to determine the scope of the immunity conferred, not by the character of the federal project or the purposes it serves, but by the character of the waters that cause the relevant damage and the purposes behind their release."[121] Accordingly, the Flood Control bars suit whenever floods or floodwaters that were or were not contained in a flood control project allegedly cause personal injury, death,[122] or property damage.[123]

The Prison Litigation Reform Act bars current prisoners from suing for mental and emotional injuries "suffered while in custody without a prior showing of physical injury."[124] The statute applies only while the prisoner remains incarcerated.[125] The "physical injury" requirement may be satisfied by a "less-than-significant-but-more-than-de minimis physical injury as a predicate to allegations of emo-

---

118. 33 U.S.C. § 702c.

119. United States v. James, 478 U.S. 597, 599–601, 612 (1986). In dicta the Court stated, "Congress clearly sought to ensure beyond doubt that sovereign immunity would protect the Government from 'any' liability associated with flood control." *Id.* at 608 (citing Nat'l Mfg. Co. v. United States, 210 F.2d 263, 270 (8th Cir. 1954)).

120. Cent. Green Co. v. United States, 531 U.S. 425, 436–37 (2001).

121. *Id.* at 434. The Court disavowed the *James* dicta discussed *supra* note 119.

122. *James*, 478 U.S. at 608.

123. *See, e.g.*, Cent. Green Co. v. United States, 531 U.S. 425, 436–37 (2001).

124. 28 U.S.C. § 1346(b)(2). The statute, enacted in 1996, bars suit by prisoners for mental or emotional injury unless accompanied by a physical injury. It states:

> No person convicted of a felony who is incarcerated while awaiting sentencing or while serving a sentence may bring a civil action against the United States or an agency, officer, or employee of the Government, for mental or emotional injury suffered while in custody without a prior showing of physical injury.

125. *See generally* Kerr v. Puckett, 138 F.3d 321, 323 (7th Cir. 1998) (noting "Congress deemed prisoners to be pestiferous litigants because they have so much free time on their hands and there are few costs to filing suit.").

tional injury."[126] The Prison Litigation Reform Act operates effectively as an exception to the law enforcement proviso of § 2680(h).[127]

Other statutes have similar explicit bars to suit. For example, 10 U.S.C. § 456 prohibits any claim "brought against the United States on the basis of the content of a navigational aid prepared or disseminated by the National Geospatial-Intelligence Agency."[128] The Panama Canal Act of 1979 blocks any suit against the United States or the Panama Canal Commission except those involving ships in transit.[129]

The Anti-Assignment Act presents a different sort of absolute bar. It prohibits any transfer or assignment of any claim against the United States until after the "claim is allowed, the amount . . . is

---

126. *See* Perez v. United States, 2008 U.S. Dist. LEXIS 42906, at *5–6 (M.D. Pa. May 30, 2008) (holding immediate effects of asthma attack were de minimis) (internal citations omitted).

127. *See* discussion *supra* notes 62–63.

128. 10 U.S.C. § 456. Civil actions barred:

> (a) Claims barred. No civil action may be brought against the United States on the basis of the content of a navigational aid prepared or disseminated by the National Geospatial-Intelligence Agency.

> (b) Navigational aids covered. Subsection (a) applies with respect to a navigational aid in the form of a map, a chart, or a publication and any other form or medium of product or information in which the National Geospatial-Intelligence Agency prepares or disseminates navigational aids.

See Hyundai Merch. Marine Co. v. United States, 888 F. Supp. 543, 547 (S.D.N.Y. 1995), *aff'd*, 75 F.3d 134 (2d Cir. 1996) (barring admiralty suit alleging navigational chart inaccurate).

129. 22 U.S.C. § 3761.

> (d) Action for damages on claims cognizable under this chapter; action against officers or employees of United States for injuries resulting from acts outside scope of their employment. Except as provided in section 1416 of this Act [22 U.S.C. § 3776], no action for damages on claims cognizable under this chapter shall lie against the United States or the Commission, and no such action shall lie against any officer or employee of the United States. . . .

See Husted v. United States, 667 F. Supp. 831, 832 (S.D. Fla. 1985), *aff'd*, 779 F.2d 58 (11th Cir. 1985) (unpublished table decision) (dismissing FTCA auto accident suit and accepting argument that "the Panama Canal Act of 1979 . . . provides for general immunity regarding actions against the United States or its Panama Canal Commission for actions arising in the Canal Zone").

decided, and a warrant for payment . . . has been issued . . . ."[130] The Anti-Assignment Act applies to voluntary assignments but not transfers required by operation of law.[131] It prohibits assignment of tort claims against the United States.[132] It also prohibits the sale of annuities from structured settlements funded by the United States.[133]

C. Other Statutes That Bar Suit

Even in the absence of exclusivity language, where a statute assigns a particular court jurisdiction over a subject, that jurisdiction may be exclusive and bar FTCA liability. For instance, the Clean Water Act grants the U.S. Court of Federal Claims jurisdiction over claims to recover certain cleanup costs from the United States.[134] Because Con-

---

130. 31 U.S.C. §3727 Assignments of claims:

(a) In this section, "assignment" means—

(1) a transfer or assignment of any part of a claim against the United States Government or of an interest in the claim; or

(2) the authorization to receive payment for any part of the claim.

(b) An assignment may be made only after a claim is allowed, the amount of the claim is decided, and a warrant for payment of the claim has been issued . . . .

131. *See* Danielson v. United States, 416 F.2d 408, 410 (9th Cir. 1969) ("[The] statute . . . is aimed at voluntary assignments and does not affect transfers by operation of law." (citing Erwin v. United States, 97 U.S. 392 (1878))).

132. *See* United States v. Shannon, 342 U.S. 288, 293–94 (1952) (holding that FTCA suit for damaged property purchased by plaintiff violated the Anti-Assignment Act).

133. *See* Transamerica Assurance Corp. v. United States, 423 F. Supp. 2d 691, 695 (W.D. Ky. 2006), *aff'd*, TransAmerica Assurance Corp. v. Settlement Capital Corp., 489 F.3d 256, 257 (6th Cir. 2007).

134. 33 U.S.C. §1321(i)(1) Recovery of removal costs:

In any case where an owner or operator of a vessel or an onshore facility or an offshore facility from which oil or a hazardous substance is discharged in violation of subsection (b)(3) of this section acts to remove such oil or substance in accordance with regulations promulgated pursuant to this section, such owner or operator shall be entitled to recover the reasonable costs incurred in such removal upon establishing, in a suit which may be brought against the United States Government in the United States Court of Federal Claims, that such discharge was caused solely by (A) an act of God, (B) an act of war, (C) negligence on the part of the United States Government, or (D) an act or omission of a third party without regard to whether such act or omission was or was not negligent, or of any combination of the foregoing causes.

gress picked that court to resolve those claims, its jurisdiction over cleanup cost is held to be exclusive.[135] Accordingly, suits for cleanup costs cannot be brought under the FTCA.[136]

Likewise, when statutes create comprehensive remedy programs, those remedies may be held to be exclusive and to preclude suit in tort even if they do not contain exclusivity language. For example, the Civil Service Reform Act (CSRA)[137] is held to be the exclusive remedy by which federal employees can seek redress of employment-related grievances[138] or improper job actions,[139] barring FTCA liability.

> The CSRA preempts . . . FTCA claims . . . if the conduct under-lying his complaint can be challenged as "prohibited person-nel practices" within the meaning of the CSRA . . . . The CSRA defines "prohibited personnel practices" as any "personnel action" taken by someone in authority that violates one of twelve enumerated practices. 5 U.S.C. § 2302(b). "Person-nel action," in turn, is defined comprehensively to include any appointment, promotion, disciplinary or corrective

---

135. *See* Platte Pipe Line Co. v. United States, 846 F.2d 610, 612 (10th Cir. 1988) (finding when there is a potential for conflict between FTCA and Clean Water act, "Claims Court has exclusive jurisdiction"); Sea-Land Service, Inc. v. United States, 684 F.2d 871, 873 (Ct. Cl. 1982) ("the statute, therefore, clearly allocates exclusive jurisdiction of sub-section (i)(1) actions to the Court of Claims"); A/S D/S Svendborg v. United States, 726 F. Supp. 1401, 1403 (S.D.N.Y. 1987) ("The legislative history contains no suggestion that authorization to sue in any other court was contemplated.").

136. *See* Platte Pipe Line Co. v. United States, 846 F.2d 610, 611–12 (10th Cir. 1988) ("[T]he Claims Court has exclusive jurisdiction over such claims [because] . . . the intent of Congress as reflected in the Clean Water Act would be frustrated if Platte were allowed to bring an action for cleanup costs under the FTCA.").

137. Civil Service Reform Act of 1978 (CSRA), Pub. L. No. 95-454, 92 Stat. 1111 (codi-fied at scattered sections of Title 5 of the United States Code).

138. *See* Kennedy v. U.S. Postal Serv., 145 F.3d 1077, 1078 (9th Cir. 1998) (barring FTCA suit where supervisor destroyed plaintiff's records; "[f]ederal employees alleging employ-ment-related tort claims subject to the CSRA may not bring an action under the FTCA.").

139. *See* Tubesing v. United States, 810 F.3d 330, 334 (5th Cir. 2016) ("[B]ecause Tubesing is a federal employee, and due to the nature of his employment-related claims, the CSRA provides Tubesing's sole remedy against his employer."); Mangano v. United States, 529 F.3d 1243, 1247 (9th Cir. 2008) (barring FTCA suit by doctor who alleged VA discharged him in retaliation for his complaints of unprofessional conduct); Prem-achandra v. United States, 739 F.2d 392, 394 (8th Cir. 1984) (barring FTCA suit by VA employee who had been wrongly discharged and then reinstated; "Congress did intend the civil service laws to provide the sole remedy for federal employees in Premachandra's circumstances.").

action, detail, transfer, reassignment, reinstatement, restoration, reemployment, performance evaluation, pay or benefits decision, mandatory psychiatric examination, or any other significant change in duties, responsibilities, or working conditions. 5 U.S.C. § 2302(a)(2)(A)(i)-(xi).[140]

The Prison Industries Fund[141] that creates a workers' compensation–type remedy for federal prisoners, is held to be the exclusive, non-FTCA remedy for prisoners injured while working in prison industries.[142] In a similar vein, the existence of a comprehensive system of benefits and support for military servicemembers was a key factor in the Supreme Court's *Feres* decision, holding that the FTCA did not waive sovereign immunity for claims arising incident to military service.[143]

---

140. *Mangano*, 529 F.3d at 1247.

141. 18 U.S.C. § 4126.

142. *See* United States v. Demko, 385 U.S. 149, 152 (1966); Vander v. U.S. Dep't of Justice, 268 F.3d 661, 663 (9th Cir. 2001):

> The Prison Industries Fund may be used to compensate "inmates . . . for injuries suffered in any industry or in any work activity in connection with the maintenance or operation of the institution in which the inmates are confined." 18 U.S.C. § 4126(c). That is the sole source of compensation for the injury; its remedy is exclusive.

Prisoners can sue under the FTCA for injuries they incur outside their Prison Industries workplace. *See* United States v. Muniz, 374 U.S. 150 (1963); Plummer v. United States, 580, 158 F.2d 72, 77 (3d Cir. 1978) (allowing suit for mental suffering by eight prisoners who contracted tuberculosis from a prisoner who had the disease).

143. Feres v. United States, 340 U.S. 135, 142, 145 (1950). *See also supra* Chapter 3.B.

CHAPTER 5

The Administrative Claims Process: Procedural Prerequisites to Making a Tort Claim

Congress established an administrative procedure by which the agency involved can settle tort claims against the government without litigation.[1] The Department of Justice, as the agency charged with administering the FTCA,[2] has promulgated regulations regarding the submission and resolution of FTCA claims.[3] This is a real remedy; the majority of FTCA administrative claims are resolved at the administrative level and do not go to litigation.[4] A claimant cannot file suit under the FTCA until it has exhausted these administrative procedures.[5]

The process for initiating the administrative claims process is simple. The FTCA requires the presentation of the claim to the "appropriate Federal agency"[6] within two years of the claim's accrual.[7] To meet the presentation requirement the claimant must, at a minimum,

---

1. 28 U.S.C. § 2675 (2012).
2. 28 U.S.C. § 2672.
3. 28 C.F.R. § 14 (2017) (attached at Appendix C). Agencies have authority to issue their own FTCA regulations. *See* 28 C.F.R. § 14.11.
4. *See* Lester S. Jayson & Robert C. Longstreth, Handling Federal Tort Claims § 17.01 (2018); Jeffrey Axelrad, *Federal Tort Claims Act Administrative Claims: Better Than Third Party ADR for Resolving Federal Tort Claims*, 52 Admin. L. Rev. 1331, 1342–45 (2000) (arguing that the administrative claim system is efficient because it enables many claims to be settled before reaching court).
5. 28 U.S.C. § 2675(a) ("An action shall not be instituted . . . unless the claimant shall have first presented the claim to the appropriate Federal agency.").
6. 28 U.S.C. §§ 2401(b), 2675(a).
7. 28 U.S.C. § 2401(b); *see infra*, Chapter 6.C. (discussing statute of limitations).

file a written claim with the agency whose "actions gave rise to the claim"[8] that states a sum certain of the damages suffered[9] and identifies the conduct involved.[10] More information may be required in some circuits.[11] The government has a special form for Federal Tort Claims, SF-95, that asks for all the required information.[12] Use of SF-95 is not mandatory.[13] The owner of damaged property, an injured person, the representative of an estate, an insurer with subrogation rights, or their agents or legal representatives can present the administrative claim.[14]

Once a claim has been properly filed, the claimant and the agency can engage informally in negotiating a settlement. In assessing a claim the agency can use alternative dispute resolution techniques and will consider, *inter alia*, the factual and legal merits of the claim and its litigative risk.[15] As is typical in tort settlement discussions, the agency will seek information to justify a claim.[16]

There is a split of authority as to whether a claimant can exhaust its FTCA administrative remedy if it fails to provide information

---

8. 28 C.F.R. § 14.2(b)(1); *see* 28 U.S.C. §§ 2401(b), 2675(a); *see also* Gonzalez v. United States, 284 F.3d 281, 291–92 (1st Cir. 2002) (barring childbirth negligence suit under FTCA for failure to file administrative claim even though plaintiff did not know that employees of federally supported health center were deemed to be federal employees for FTCA purposes); Hart v. Dep't of Labor *ex rel.* United States, 116 F.3d 1338, 1341 (10th Cir. 1997) (affirming dismissal of plaintiff's claim because the completed administrative claim was filed on last day of limitations period with the Attorney General rather than the Department of Labor).

9. 28 C.F.R. § 14.2(a); *see* 28 U.S.C. § 2675(b); Millares Guiraldes de Tineo v. United States, 137 F.3d 715, 720 (2d Cir. 1998) (holding that purported administrative claim of DEA informant who had been incarcerated in Chile "failed to meet the FTCA's requirements because it did not mention any specific sum of money").

10. *See, e.g.*, Tidd v. United States, 786 F.2d 1565, 1566, 1568 (11th Cir. 1986) (barring suit arising from "swine flu vaccination received on October 21, 1976, in Jefferson County, Alabama" where the administrative claim "designated the 'accident' as having occurred in Maylene, Alabama, on December 5, 1976").

11. *See infra* text at notes 17–22.

12. A copy of this form can be found in Appendix D. A fillable PDF version is available at https://www.gsa.gov/cdnstatic/SF95-07a.pdf?forceDownload=1.

13. *See* Williams v. United States, 693 F.2d 555, 557–58 (5th Cir. 1982).

14. 28 C.F.R. § 14.3.

15. 28 C.F.R. § 14.6(a)–(b).

16. *See* 28 C.F.R. § 14.4 (setting out categories of information to be provided by claimant).

required by the Department of Justice's administrative claims regulations beyond a sum certain and identification of the tortious conduct.[17] In *Kanar v. United States* the Seventh Circuit required compliance with the 28 C.F.R. § 14.2(a) regulation that requires: "(i) notification of the incident; (ii) a demand for a sum certain; (iii) the title or capacity of the person signing; and (iv) evidence of this person's authority to represent the claimant."[18] The issue was whether the administrative claim requirement was met where Long, the claimant's attorney, failed to give the agency evidence of his authority to represent the claimant when requested to do so.[19] The court affirmed dismissal on grounds that the claim was invalid, even though it identified the tortious conduct and stated a sum certain, because the agency's decision to close the file was "a reasonable response to the disdain of a reasonable request. As a result, the settlement process that Congress created as a prelude to litigation was thwarted. Long's omission was not harmless; it scotched the process."[20] The Eighth, Ninth, Eleventh, and D.C. Circuits require less cooperation from the claimant:[21] "To conflate the mandatory presentment requirement . . . with the settlement procedures . . . and require claimants to substantiate claims for settlement purposes as a prerequisite to filing suit, is to compel compliance with settlement procedures contrary to congressional intent."[22]

---

17. *See* Jayson & Longstreth, *supra* note 4, § 17.09.

18. *See* Kanar v. United States, 118 F.3d 527, 528 (7th Cir. 1997).

19. *Id.* at 528.

20. *Id.* at 531 (citing McNeil v. United States, 508 U.S. 103, 106 (1993)); *see also* Mader v. United States, 619 F.3d 996 (8th Cir. 2010) (declining to adopt the reasoning of *Kanar*), *aff'd en banc* 09-1025, 2011 WL 3903256 (8th Cir. Sept. 7, 2011).

21. *See generally* Tidd v. United States, 786 F.2d. 1565, 1567 (11th Cir. 1986) ("Although a claimant has an obligation to give notice of a claim under § 2675, he or she does not have an obligation to provide further information to assist *settlement* of the matter." (citing Adams v. United States, 615 F.2d 284, 289 (5th Cir. 1980), *clarified on denial of reh'g*, 622 F.2d 197 (1980))). *See generally* Farmers State Sav. Bank v. Farmers Home Admin., 866 F.2d 276, 277 (8th Cir. 1989) (citing cases); GAF Corp. v. United States, 818 F.2d 901, 919–20 (D.C. Cir. 1987); Warren v. U.S. Dep't of Interior Bureau of Land Mgmt., 724 F.2d 776, 778 (9th Cir. 1984) (en banc) ("We find the relevant statutes and their legislative histories reveal that Congress did not intend to treat regulations promulgated pursuant to [§] 2672 as jurisdictional prerequisites under [§] 2675(a).").

22. *GAF Corp*, 818 F.2d at 919.

If a proposed settlement exceeds the agency's settlement authority, authority to enter the settlement must be obtained from the Department of Justice.[23] Once a proposed settlement has been approved it will be submitted for payment under the procedures outlined in Chapter 10.

---

23. 28 C.F.R. § 14.6(b)–(e). Absent a delegation of greater authority an agency has $25,000 in settlement authority. *See* 28 C.F.R. § 14.10. The Department of Justice has delegated greater authority to some agencies that handle numerous claims. *See id.* and the Appendix to 28 C.F.R. Part 14—Delegations of Settlement Authority.

CHAPTER 6

Procedural Requirements in FTCA Litigation

A. Exhaustion of Administrative Remedies

Suit cannot be filed until the claimant has exhausted its remedies under the FTCA's administrative claims procedure.[1] Administrative exhaustion can occur if the agency either denies the claim "in writing," or it fails to dispose of the claim "within six months after it is filed . . . ."[2] If suit is filed before the claim is denied or six months have passed, it will be dismissed.[3] In *McNeil v. United States*, where a pro se plaintiff filed suit four months before filing his administrative claim, the Supreme Court unanimously affirmed dismissal, explaining that "[t]he FTCA bars claimants from bringing suit in federal court until they have exhausted their administrative remedies."[4] As a consequence, there can be no class action suits under the FTCA

---

1. 28 U.S.C. §2675(a) (2012). The administrative exhaustion requirement does not apply "to such claims as may be asserted under the Federal Rules of Civil Procedure by third party complaint, cross-claim, or counterclaim." *Id.*

2. *Id.*

3. *See* Robles v. Beaufort Mem'l Hosp., 482 F. Supp. 2d 700, 706 (D.S.C. 2007) (dismissing for failure to exhaust and noting, "[t]his court cannot stay Plaintiff's case pending exhaustion of her administrative remedies").

4. McNeil v. United States, 508 U.S. 106, 113 (1993). The Court reasoned:

> The most natural reading of the statute indicates that Congress intended to require complete exhaustion of Executive remedies before invocation of the judicial process. Every premature filing of an action under the FTCA imposes some burden on the judicial system and on the Department of Justice which must assume the defense of such actions. Although the burden may be slight in an individual case, the statute governs the processing of a vast multitude of claims. The interest in orderly administration of this body of litigation is best served by adherence to the straightforward statutory command.

> *Id.* at 112–13 (footnote omitted).

unless all the class participants have filed administrative claims and had them denied or left unresolved for six months.[5]

Congress created an exception to the exhaustion requirement for claims asserted "by third party complaint, cross-claim, or counter-claim" under the Federal Rules of Civil Procedure.[6] The exhaustion exception for crossclaims typically arises "where the United States and another party are joined as defendants, as joint tortfeasors, and one or the other, or both, file a cross-claim against the other for con-tribution or indemnity" under Federal Rule of Civil Procedure 13.[7] For FTCA exhaustion purposes a counterclaim must be a compulsory counterclaim within the meaning of Federal Rule of Civil Procedure 13(a).[8] Similarly, a third party complaint will fall within the excep-tion to the exhaustion requirement only to the extent it seeks con-tribution or indemnity from the government.[9] This is an extremely complex area that warrants special attention.

---

5. *See, e.g.*, Lunsford v. United States, 570 F.2d 221, 229 (8th Cir. 1977) (affirming dismissal of unnamed persons in class action suit for failure to file an administrative claim following flood that resulted from cloud seeding); *see also* Dalrymple v. United States, 460 F.3d 1318, 1325 (11th Cir. 2006) (requiring compliance with sum certain requirement in suit arising from execution of warrants regarding custody of Cuban child-refugee Elian Gonzalez, "because each claimant must independently satisfy the prerequisite for filing suit under the FTCA by providing a sum certain claim, . . . the other ninety-seven claim-ants who filed a sum certain claim do not satisfy the statutory prerequisite for the [four] dismissed plaintiffs who omitted a sum certain in their claims.").

6. 28 U.S.C. § 2675(a) ("The provisions of this subsection [requiring administrative exhaustion] shall not apply to such claims as may be asserted under the Federal Rules of Civil Procedure by third party complaint, cross-claim, or counterclaim.").

7. Lester S. Jayson & Robert C. Longstreth, Handling Federal Tort Claims § 5.11[2] (2018).

8. *See* Spawr v. United States, 796 F.2d 279, 281 (9th Cir. 1986); Jayson & Longstreth, *supra* note 7, § 5.11[1].

9. Keene Corp. v. United States, 700 F.2d 836, 842–43 (2d Cir. 1983) ("We perceive no reason to read the FTCA's reference to third party actions as including more than is encompassed by Rule 14."); Jayson & Longstreth, *supra* note 7, § 17.01.

B. Courts, Juries, and Parties

Only federal district courts have subject matter jurisdiction over FTCA cases.[10] Venue is proper only in a federal district where "plaintiff resides or wherein the act or omission complained of occurred."[11] The FTCA venue provision can be waived.[12] There is no right to a jury trial under the FTCA; all cases are tried to the bench.[13] Only the United States can be sued under the FTCA;[14] the Act does not provide a vehicle for suing individuals[15] or federal agencies.[16]

C. The FTCA's Statutes of Limitations

The FTCA has two statutes of limitations. One requires that the administrative claim be presented in writing to the appropriate Federal agency within two years after the claim accrues.[17] A claim accrues when the claimant is "in possession of the critical facts that he has been hurt and who has inflicted the injury."[18] Accrual is not delayed until the claimant knows that there was tortious conduct.[19] The

---

10. 28 U.S.C. § 1346(b); Whisnant v. United States, 400 F.3d 1177, 1180 (9th Cir. 2005) (explaining that the FTCA confers subject matter jurisdiction on federal district courts to hear tort actions against the government for the negligence of its employees) (citing 28 U.S.C. § 1346(b)).

11. 28 U.S.C. § 1402(b); Simpson v. Fed. Bureau of Prisons, 496 F. Supp. 2d 187, 193 (D.D.C. 2007) (finding venue improper where plaintiff, a resident of Virginia, alleged medical malpractice at prison in Pennsylvania); *see also* Reuber v. United States, 750 F.2d 1039, 1047–48 (D.C. Cir. 1984) (affirming dismissal of FTCA claim because the plaintiff, a resident of Maryland where the alleged tortious act occurred, could point to no act or omission in the District of Columbia, where plaintiff filed suit) *rev'd on other grounds*, Kauffman v. Anglo-Am. Sch. of Sofia, 28 F.3d 1223 (D.C. Cir. 1994).

12. *See* Upchurch v. Piper Aircraft Corp., 736 F.2d 439, 440 (8th Cir. 1984) (holding United States waived venue objection by not including it in answer).

13. 28 U.S.C. § 2402 (an FTCA suit "shall be tried by the court without a jury").

14. 28 U.S.C. § 1346(b); *see also* 28 U.S.C. § 2679(d)(1).

15. *See* Smith v. United States, 561 F.3d 1090, 1099 (10th Cir. 2009) ("The United States is the only proper defendant in an FTCA action.").

16. *See* Allen v. Veterans Admin., 749 F.2d 1386, 1388 (9th Cir. 1984).

17. 28 U.S.C. § 2401(b) (2012); *see, e.g.,* Garrett v. United States, 640 F.2d 24, 26 (6th Cir. 1981) (holding claim for wrongful death of prisoner accrued on day he died, not on day Bureau of Prisons released autopsy report).

18. United States v. Kubrick, 444 U.S. 111, 122 (1979) (medical malpractice); *see also* Indus. Constructors Corp. v. U.S. Bureau of Reclamation, 15 F.3d 963, 968 (10th Cir. 1994) (rejecting argument that filing administrative claim would have been futile).

19. *See Kubrick*, 444 U.S. at 123–24; Jayson & Longstreth, *supra* note 7, § 14.03.

second FTCA statute of limitations requires that suit be filed within six months of the agency's denial of the administrative claim.[20] State law tolling doctrines such as those for infancy[21] or incompetency[22] do not apply to the FTCA statutes of limitations.

In 2015 the Supreme Court held in *United States v. Kwai Fun Wong*[23] that the FTCA statutes of limitations are procedural in nature rather than jurisdictional. It further held they are subject to equitable tolling.[24] The test to be applied to determine equitable tolling in FTCA cases has not been resolved. The *Kwai Fun Wong* opinion noted that equitable tolling is available in private litigation when a party diligently pursued his rights but was prevented from meeting a deadline by an extraordinary circumstance.[25] The next year, in *Menominee Indian Tribe of Wisconsin v. United States*,[26] a Contract Disputes Act case, the Court affirmed a decision that had applied the two-part test for equitable tolling established for habeas corpus cases in *Holland v. Florida*.[27] Under that test a plaintiff must show "(1) that he has been pursuing his rights diligently, and (2) that some extraordinary circumstance stood in his way and prevented timely filing."[28] In *Menominee*, the Court noted it had never held that the *Holland* test

---

20. 28 U.S.C. § 2401(b); Willis v. United States, 719 F.2d 608, 612–13 (2d Cir. 1983) (suit barred by six-month limitations period even though suit filed less than two years after auto accident). *See generally* McNeil v. United States, 508 U.S. 106 (1993).

21. *See, e.g.*, T.L. *ex rel.* Ingram v. United States, 443 F.3d 956, 965 (8th Cir. 2006); MacMillan v. United States, 46 F.3d 377, 381 (5th Cir. 1995) (citing Zavala v. United States, 876 F.2d 780, 782 (9th Cir. 1989)) ("[U]nder the FTCA, the limitations period is not tolled during the minority of the putative plaintiff; rather 'his parent's knowledge of the injuries is imputed to him.'").

22. *See, e.g.*, Chomic v. United States, 377 F.3d 607, 615 (6th Cir. 2004) ("[C]ourts have uniformly held that mental incompetency, standing alone, will not toll the running of the statute of limitations under the FTCA.").

23. United States v. Kwai Fun Wong, 135 S. Ct. 1625, 1638 (2015).

24. *Id.* The *Kwai Fun Wong* opinion resolved two cases: Kwai Fun Wong v. Beebe, 732 F.3d 1030, 1033 (9th Cir. 2013), involving the FTCA's six-month limitations period, and June v. United States, 550 F. App'x 505, 506 (9th Cir. 2013), involving its two-year limitations period.

25. *Kwai Fun Wong*, 135 S. Ct. at 1631.

26. Menominee Indian Tribe of Wis. v. United States, 136 S. Ct. 750 (2016).

27. Holland v. Florida, 560 U.S. 631, 649 (2010).

28. *Id.* (quoted in *Menominee*, 136 S. Ct. at 755).

applies "outside the habeas context."[29] In the absence of definitive guidance, circuit courts have applied different tests in FTCA cases.[30] Whatever the test, plaintiffs face an uphill struggle to succeed with equitable estoppel arguments.[31]

---

29. 136 S. Ct. at 756 n.2 ("Nevertheless, because we agree that the Tribe cannot meet *Holland's* test, we have no occasion to decide whether an even stricter test might apply to a nonhabeas case.").

30. *E.g., compare* Poppe v. United States, 690 F. App'x 480, 481 (9th Cir. 2017) (applying *Holland* test in FTCA case), *and* Raplee v. United States, 842 F.3d 328, 333 (4th Cir. 2016) (same), *with* Zappone v. United States, 870 F.3d 551, 557 (6th Cir. 2017) (declining to apply Holland test in FTCA case; instead applying five-part Sixth Circuit test).

31. *See, e.g.,* cases cited in note 30 (all denying equitable tolling).

CHAPTER 7

Government Employee Defendants & the FTCA

Federal employees who commit tortious acts have special protections from personal liability. The FTCA provides two distinct, important defenses for them. First, in § 2679 it creates complete statutory immunity for federal employees from tort liability arising from acts or omissions within the scope of their federal employment[1] unless the claim is based on a violation of the Constitution or of a federal statute that creates a cause of action against individuals.[2] This immunity

---

1. 28 U.S.C. § 2679(b), (d) (2012).

(b) (1) The remedy against the United States provided by [the FTCA] for injury or loss of property, or personal injury or death arising or resulting from the negligent or wrongful act or omission of any employee of the Government while acting within the scope of his office or employment is exclusive of any other civil action or proceeding for money damages by reason of the same subject matter against the employee whose act or omission gave rise to the claim or against the estate of such employee. Any other civil action or proceeding for money damages arising out of or relating to the same subject matter against the employee or the employee's estate is precluded without regard to when the act or omission occurred.

28 U.S.C. § 2679(b)(1). These procedures were enacted in the Federal Employees Liability Reform and Tort Compensation Act of 1988 (the Westfall Act), Congress's response to Westfall v. Erwin, 484 U.S. 292, 296–97 (1988) (holding that federal employees are immune from suit for common law torts only if they were acting within the scope of employment and were exercising discretionary functions).

2. 28 U.S.C. § 2679(b)(2) states:

(2) Paragraph (1) does not extend or apply to a civil action against an employee of the Government—

(A) which is brought for a violation of the Constitution of the United States, or

(B) which is brought for a violation of a statute of the United States under which such action against an individual is otherwise authorized.

applies regardless of whether the plaintiff has a viable claim under the FTCA.[3] Second, § 2676 provides a complete defense to any suit against a federal employee if an FTCA judgment has been entered "by reason of the same subject matter."[4] Finally, though not expressed in the FTCA, federal employees cannot be sued by the United States for indemnity even if their negligence resulted in an FTCA judgment and state law would allow a private employer to bring such a claim against its employee.[5]

The substitution and dismissal provisions of § 2679 do not apply to suits alleging violations of the Constitution or some federal statutes.[6] Accordingly, when federal employees are sued under *Bivens*[7] for Constitutional torts the FTCA does not authorize substitution and dismissal of the individual federal defendants. While *Bivens* litigation is beyond the scope of this book, it is important that employees sued in such cases be aware that the government may provide legal representation to them.[8] Any employee who desires or may be entitled to representation in such a case should immediately send a written request for representation along with all pleading and process documents to his or her immediate supervisor or the officer designated by the agency to receive such requests.[9]

A. Substitution & Dismissal under § 2679

The Department of Justice has initial responsibility for deciding whether the defendant was a federal employee acting within the

---

3. *See* United States v. Smith, 499 U.S. 160, 166–67 (1991) (holding FTCA renders federal employee tortfeasors immune from suit even when FTCA defenses bar recovery).
4. 28 U.S.C. § 2676.
5. *See* United States v. Gilman, 347 U.S. 507, 511 (1954). *But cf.* Grant v. United States, 271 F.2d 651 (2d Cir. 1959) (allowing government claim for indemnity from employee's insurer); United States v. Merchs. Mut. Ins. Co., 2007 U.S. Dist. LEXIS 45454, at *16 (D.N.J. June 22, 2007) (allowing government claim for indemnity from insurer in slip and fall case at Merchant Marine Academy officers' club).
6. *See* 28 U.S.C. § 2679(b)(2).
7. Bivens v. Six Unknown Named Agents of Fed. Bureau of Narcotics, 403 U.S. 388, 396 (1971).
8. *See* 28 C.F.R. § 50.15. [Attached as Appendix C.4.]
9. *Id.* § 50.15(a)(1).

scope of employment at the time of the event giving rise to the suit[10] if the suit is one to which § 2679 applies.[11] Under the Act's procedures the employee who has been sued must promptly deliver copies of all the legal pleadings and process papers to his immediate supervisor or the person designated at his agency to receive such papers.[12] The supervisor or agency officer will forward copies of those papers to the United States Attorney, the Attorney General, and the head of the agency.[13] The agency will then prepare a report regarding whether the defendant employee was acting within the scope of employment and send copies of it to the U.S. Attorney for the district in which the action is pending and to the Torts Branch, Civil Division, U.S. Department of Justice.[14] The U.S. Attorney or a Director of the Torts Branch will then decide whether to certify that the defendant employee was acting within the scope of employment.[15] The scope of employment issue for purposes of § 2679 is identical to the scope of employment issue under § 1346(b)(1),[16] turning on the respondeat superior law of the state in which the negligent or wrongful act occurred.[17]

If the Department of Justice concludes the employee was acting within the scope of employment, it will certify that conclusion.[18] If the case is in state court it will be removed to the federal district court where the action was pending.[19] The United States will then be substituted as defendant and the employee will be dismissed.[20] If the

---

10. *See* 28 U.S.C. § 2679(d); 28 C.F.R. § 15.4(a)–(b)(2010).

11. That is, a tort suit not alleging violation of the Constitution or a federal statute that creates a cause of action. *See* 28 U.S.C. § 2679(b)(2). In making its decision the Department of Justice will consider the views of the employing agency. *See* 28 C.F.R. § 15.3.

12. *See* 28 U.S.C. § 2679(c); 28 C.F.R. § 15.2.

13. *See* 28 U.S.C. § 2679(c).

14. *See* 28 C.F.R. § 15.3.

15. *See* 28 C.F.R. § 15.4(a)–(b).

16. *See* discussion at pages 17–18 *supra*.

17. *See* Williams v. United States, 350 U.S. 857, 857 (1955) (per curiam); *see also* discussion at pages 17–18 *supra*.

18. *See* 28 U.S.C. § 2679(d); 28 C.F.R. § 15.4(a)–(b). The case will then proceed under the FTCA. *See* 28 U.S.C. § 2679(d)(4).

19. *See* 28 U.S.C. § 2679(d)(2). The case cannot be remanded to state court even if the certification of scope of employment is reversed. *See* Osborn v. Haley, 549 U.S. 225, 231–32 (2007) (holding "once certification and removal are effected, exclusive competence to adjudicate the case resides in the federal court").

20. *See* 28 U.S.C. § 2679(d)(1).

United States is substituted as defendant the suit will not be barred by limitations if it "would have been timely had it been filed on the date the underlying civil action was commenced," and an administrative claim "is presented to the appropriate Federal agency within 60 days after dismissal of the civil actions."[21]

If the Department of Justice refuses to certify that the employee was acting within the scope of employment the employee may petition the court to issue the certification.[22] The Department also has authority to withdraw a certification.[23] If the Department of Justice does certify that the employee was acting within the scope of employment, another party may challenge that decision in federal district court.[24] In evaluating the scope of employment issue the district court is not limited to the allegations of the complaint,[25] and has discretion to allow discovery.[26] A court order rejecting the Attorney General's certification is subject to immediate appellate review under the collateral order doctrine.[27]

B. The Judgment Bar of § 2676

Section 2676 provides, "The judgment in an action under section 1346(b) of this title shall constitute a complete bar to any action by the claimant, by reason of the same subject matter, against the employee of the government whose act or omission gave rise to the

---

21. *See* 28 U.S.C. § 2679(d)(5).

22. *See* 28 U.S.C. § 2679(d)(3).

23. *See* 28 C.F.R. § 15.4(c).

24. *See* Gutierrez De Martinez v. Lamagno, 515 U.S. 417, 436–37 (1995).

25. *See* Osborn v. Haley, 549 U.S. 225, 231 (2007) (holding that the United States would remain as the substituted defendant "unless and until the District Court determines that the employee, *in fact*, and not simply as alleged by the plaintiff, engaged in conduct beyond the scope of his employment").

26. *See, e.g.*, Borneman v. United States, 213 F.3d 819, 827 (4th Cir. 2000); *see also* LESTER S. JAYSON & ROBERT C. LONGSTRETH, HANDLING FEDERAL TORT CLAIMS § 6.01(c) (2018) (providing a detailed discussion of the procedural nuances of challenges to certification decisions).

27. *See Osborn*, 549 U.S. at 238–39.

claim."[28] When it enacted this section Congress intended to prevent both multiple recoveries and multiple lawsuits.[29] The law regarding the § 2676 bar is clear on several points. The bar applies when an FTCA judgment is entered against the United States and a federal employee is sued in a subsequent suit arising from the same facts.[30] If the subsequent claim arises from different facts the bar does not apply.[31] Nor does it apply if judgment was entered for the United States because one of the FTCA exceptions applied.[32] There is no right to appeal immediately the denial of a judgment bar defense.[33]

Other aspects of § 2676 jurisprudence are less settled. While the majority of courts hold that § 2676 applies to suits against individual federal defendants that are pending contemporaneously with FTCA suits,[34] there is a contrary view.[35] This is a complex area that warrants careful attention.[36]

---

28. 28 U.S.C. § 2676. A similar provision applies to administrative settlements. 28 U.S.C. § 2672:

> The acceptance by the claimant of any such award, compromise, or settlement shall be final and conclusive on the claimant, and shall constitute a complete release of any claim against the United States and against the employee of the government whose act or omission gave rise to the claim, by reason of the same subject matter.

29. *See Hearings on H.R. 5373 and H.R. 6463 Before H. Comm. on the Judiciary,* 77th Cong., 2d Sess. at 9 (Statement of Ass't Att'y Gen. Francis M. Shea) (discussing government burden of defending truck driver after paying FTCA judgment or claim); *see also* Hoosier Bancorp of Ind., Inc. v. Rasmussen, 90 F.3d 180, 184 (7th Cir. 1996); Gasho v. United States, 39 F.3d 1420, 1437 (9th Cir. 1994).

30. *See* Armstrong v. Vogel, 424 F. Supp. 445, 447 (D.S.C. 1977).

31. *See, e.g.,* Unus v. Kane, 565 F.3d 103, 122 (4th Cir. 2009) (barring *Bivens* claims against federal employee defendants identified in companion FTCA claim, but allowing *Bivens* claims against other federal employee defendants whose actions were not alleged in the FTCA claim).

32. *See* Simmons v. Himmelreich, 136 S. Ct. 1843, 1850 (2016) (holding that "The judgment bar provision . . . does not apply to the categories of claims in the 'Exceptions' sections of the FTCA.").

33. *See* Will v. Hallock, 546 U.S. 345, 355 (2006).

34. *See, e.g.,* Manning v. United States, 546 F.3d 430, 433 (7th Cir. 2008); Estate of Trentadue *ex rel.* Aguilar v. United States, 397 F.3d 840, 859 (10th Cir. 2005) (applying § 2676 to bar previously entered *Bivens* judgment).

35. *See* Kreines v. United States, 959 F.2d 834, 838 (9th Cir. 1992) (holding contemporaneous claim not barred).

36. *See* Jayson & Longstreth, *supra* note 26, at § 16.13 (discussing cases).

CHAPTER 8

Damages

Because the FTCA provides that "[t]he United States shall be liable, respecting . . . tort claims, in the same manner and to the same extent as a private individual under like circumstances,"[1] FTCA awards are governed in most respects by state damages law. This general rule is qualified by specific limits Congress included in the FTCA. First no award can exceed the amount claimed administratively, absent newly discovered evidence or intervening facts.[2] Second, the Act bars punitive damages.[3] Third, it prohibits pre-judgment interest[4] and limits post judgment interest.[5]

---

1. 28 U.S.C. §2674 (2012) ("The United States shall be liable, respecting the provisions of this title relating to tort claims, in the same manner and to the same extent as a private individual under like circumstances, but shall not be liable for interest prior to judgment or for punitive damages."); *accord* 28 U.S.C. § 1346(b)(1).
2. 28 U.S.C. §2675(b).
3. 28 U.S.C. §2674.
4. *Id.*
5. *See infra* Chapter 9.D. (discussion of post-judgment interest).

A. Assessing Damages

"Under the Federal Tort Claims Act, damages are determined by the law of the State where the tortious act was committed . . . ."[6] Accordingly, in FTCA cases, state law will provide the elements of damages,[7] and the rules requiring mitigation of damages,[8] reducing damages because of plaintiff's comparative fault,[9] and discounting future damages to present value.[10] Some older cases suggested that the FTCA's proscription of punitive damages under 28 U.S.C. § 2674 might require rejection of the total offset method in spite of state law authorizing its use.[11] In light of the Supreme Court's decision in *Molzof*[12] that analysis is foreclosed.[13]

---

6. *See* Hatahley v. United States, 351 U.S. 173, 182 (1956); *accord* Molzof v. United States, 502 U.S. 301, 305 (1992). The FTCA's one exception is if state law provides for only punitive damages in wrongful death cases.

> If, however, in any case where in death was caused, the law of the place where the act or omission complained of occurred provides, or has been construed to provide, for damages only punitive in nature, the United States shall be liable for actual or compensatory damages, measured by the pecuniary injuries resulting from such death to the persons respectively, for whose benefit the action was brought, in lieu thereof.

28 U.S.C. § 2674. *See generally* Mass. Bonding & Ins. Co. v. United States, 352 U.S. 128, 133–34 (1956) (holding entire body of Massachusetts wrongful death law, including cap on punitive damages, inapplicable).

7. *See*, e.g., Neyer v. United States, 845 F.2d 641, 646–47 (6th Cir. 1988) (remanding for further analysis under Ohio law an award for loss of homemaker services); Litif v. United States, 682 F. Supp. 2d 60, 83–85 (D. Mass. 2010) (discussing loss of consortium under Massachusetts law).

8. *See* LaMarca v. United States, 31 F. Supp. 2d 110, 131 (E.D.N.Y. 1998).

9. *See, e.g.*, Yeary v. United States, 754 F. Supp. 546, 553 (E.D. Mich. 1991) (applying Michigan's pure comparative negligence standard in pedestrian-postal vehicle case, court reduced damages by forty percent).

10. *See, e.g.*, Lucas v. United States, 807 F.2d 414, 422 (5th Cir. 1986) (applying Texas law); MacDonald v. United States, 781 F. Supp. 320, 325 (M.D. Pa. 1991), *aff'd*, 983 F.2d 1051 (3d Cir. 1992) (noting "the FTCA defers to state law on the substantive issue of liability as well as on the computation of damages . . . . The Supreme Court of Pennsylvania has specifically held that, as a matter of law, inflation is offset by interest, thereby negating the need to discount to present value.").

11. *See* Scott v. United States, 884 F.2d 1280, 1285 (9th Cir. 1989); Hollinger v. United States, 651 F.2d 636, 642 (9th Cir. 1981).

12. Molzof v. United States, 502 U.S. 301, 305 (1992).

13. *See* discussion *infra* at notes 43–46.

State legislative caps on damages apply to FTCA judgments.[14] The United States has the benefit of such damages caps even if it does not comply with all the procedures and filing requirements of the state statutes that create those limits on recovery.[15] Three reasons support this result: "(1) the FTCA refers to like circumstances rather than identical circumstances, (2) the financial responsibility of the United States is assured, and (3) its failure to contribute to a compensation fund is immaterial because (unlike qualified providers) it must pay its liabilities without resort to the compensation fund."[16]

State collateral source rules generally apply under the FTCA when the collateral source is unrelated to the government.[17] Application of the collateral source rule is more complicated when federal funds have been paid to a plaintiff under a government program.

As a general matter, the test to determine whether a particular governmental payment is collateral to an FTCA judgment focuses on whether the claimant has contributed to the fund from which the benefit is paid. Payments that come from unfunded general revenues of the United States are deductible from an FTCA award, and those that come from a special

---

14. *See* Richards v. United States, 369 U.S. 1, 16 (1962) ("It is conceded that each petitioner has received $15,000, the maximum amount recoverable [for wrongful death] under the Missouri Act, and the petitioners thus have received full compensation for their claims."); Hill v. United States, 81 F.3d 118, 121 (10th Cir. 1996) ("These cases stand for the proposition that where there is a specific cap on tort liability, the United States government may benefit from this limit although it did not otherwise participate in the statutory scheme which provides the cap.") (citing cases); Smith v. Pena, 621 F.2d 873, 881 (7th Cir. 1980) ("plaintiffs are limited by the [Illinois] Dram Shop Act's provision relating to damages," capping them at $15,000 per person injured).

15. *See* Haceesa v. United States, 309 F.3d 722, 726 (10th Cir. 2002) (applying New Mexico medical malpractice cap on damages in FTCA case) (citing Carter v. United States, 982 F.2d 1141, 1143–44 (7th Cir. 1992); Lozada v. United States, 974 F.2d 986, 987 (8th Cir. 1992); Owen v. United States, 935 F.2d 734, 737–38 (5th Cir. 1991)).

16. *Haceesa*, 309 F.3d at 726.

17. *See* Scheib v. Fla. Sanitarium & Benev. Ass'n, 759 F.2d 859, 864 (11th Cir. 1985); Douglas v. United States, 658 F.2d 445, 450 (6th Cir. 1981) ("[S]tate collateral source rules are applied in FTCA actions.") (citing Klein v. United States, 339 F.2d 512, 517–18 (2d Cir. 1964); Tyminski v. United States, 481 F.2d 257, 270 (3d Cir. 1973) (gratuitously provided nursing services); Cooper v. United States, 313 F. Supp. 1207, 1212 (D. Neb. 1970)); Calva-Cerqueira v. United States, 281 F. Supp. 2d 279, 296 (D.D.C. 2003); Coates v. United States, 612 F. Supp. 592, 597 (C.D. Ill. 1985).

fund supplied in part by the beneficiary are collateral and therefore nondeductible.[18]

Accordingly, veterans' benefits have been deducted from awards to former service members.[19] Benefits that the plaintiff has earned or contributed to, such as those provided by the Civil Service Reform Act,[20] Social Security,[21] Medicare,[22] and federal sick leave[23] are not deductible.

B. Amount Stated in Administrative Claim

FTCA damages cannot exceed the amount stated in the administrative claim, absent "newly discovered evidence not reasonably discoverable at the time of presenting the claim to the federal agency, or upon allegation and proof of intervening facts . . . ."[24] The requirement is a real bar that does keep plaintiffs from recovering damages in excess of their administrative claim unless one of the two exceptions applies.[25]

---

18. LESTER S. JAYSON & ROBERT C. LONGSTRETH, HANDLING FEDERAL TORT CLAIMS § 10.04[5] (2018) (citing Berg v. United States, 806 F.2d 978, 984–85 (10th Cir. 1986); Siverson v. United States, 710 F.2d 557, 560 (9th Cir. 1983)).

19. See JAYSON & LONGSTRETH, supra note 18, § 10.04[5] (citing, inter alia, 38 U.S.C. § 1151; United States v. Brown, 348 U.S. 110 (1954)).

20. See id. (citing, inter alia, United States v. Price, 288 F.2d 448 (4th Cir. 1961)).

21. See id. (citing, inter alia, Manko v. United States, 830 F.2d 831 (8th Cir. 1987)).

22. See id. (citing, inter alia, Titchnell v. United States, 681 F.2d 165 (3d Cir. 1982)).

23. See id. (citing, inter alia, Leeper v. United States, 756 F.2d 300 (3d Cir. 1985)).

24. 28 U.S.C. § 2675(b):

> (b) Action under this section shall not be instituted for any sum in excess of the amount of the claim presented to the federal agency, except where the increased amount is based upon newly discovered evidence not reasonably discoverable at the time of presenting the claim to the federal agency, or upon allegation and proof of intervening facts, relating to the amount of the claim.

25. Id.; see, e.g., Lebron v. United States, 279 F.3d 321, 331 (5th Cir. 2002) (remanding and limiting severely injured child's recovery to "the $20 million stated in the administrative claim"); Low v. United States, 795 F.2d 466, 470 (5th Cir. 1986) (reducing $3.5 million judgment to the $1,275,000 stated in administrative claim); Salcedo-Albanez v. United States, 149 F. Supp. 2d 1240, 1245 (S.D. Cal. 2001) (holding "[b]ecause the prospect of permanent damage to Plaintiff's optical nerve was known, Plaintiff is now barred from increasing her FTCA complaint for damages" beyond the $75,000 in her administrative claim; plaintiff lost all vision in right eye).

Courts treat the exceptions as interchangeable and apply the same tests to both.[26]

> [T]he question of whether damages could be increased under § 2675(b) present[s] a twofold issue. First, . . . [could] the post-claim evidence . . . have been discovered at the time the plaintiff filed its administrative claim? Second, do these facts represent newly discovered evidence or intervening facts for the purposes of § 2675(b)? The second prong of the analysis has several requirements. First, the evidence must support the increase in the prayer over the administrative claim. Next, the allegedly newly discovered evidence or intervening facts must not have been reasonably capable of detection at the time the administrative claim was filed.[27]

Plaintiff will be held to the amount stated in the administrative claim if conditions did not change after the claim was filed[28] or if plaintiff could have learned of the increased injury through the exercise of reasonable diligence.[29] Plaintiff has the burden of showing either newly discovered evidence or intervening facts.[30] Information that only "bear[s] out earlier suspicions" and "[d]iagnoses which are no more than cumulative and confirmatory of earlier diagnoses" are insufficient for § 2675(b) purposes.[31] The test for assessing whether newly discovered evidence or intervening facts were reasonably

---

26. *See* Daniel S. Read, *The Courts' Difficult Balancing Act to Be Fair to Both Plaintiff and Government Under the FTCA's Administrative Claims Process*, 57 BAYLOR L. REV. 785, 804 (2005).

27. Dickerson v. United States, 280 F.3d 470, 475–76 (5th Cir. 2002) (citing and quoting Low v. United States, 795 F.2d 466, 470 (5th Cir. 1986)) (internal citations and quotation marks omitted).

28. *See Lebron*, 279 F.3d at 331 (holding that plaintiffs limited to amount sought in administrative claim, where the basic severity of condition was known and stated in the administrative claim); Reilly v. United States, 863 F.2d 149, 172–73 (1st Cir. 1988); Low v. United States, 795 F.2d 466, 471 (5th Cir. 1986) ("There is no evidence that the[] conditions became worse or that other conditions developed after the claim was filed.").

29. *See* Zurba v. United States, 318 F.3d 736, 740 (7th Cir. 2003); *Low*, 795 F.2d at 470.

30. *See* Spivey v. United States, 912 F.2d 80, 85 (4th Cir. 1990); Allgeier v. United States, 909 F.2d 869, 877 (6th Cir. 1990); Kielwien v. United States, 540 F.2d 676, 680 (4th Cir. 1976).

31. Reilly v. United States, 863 F.2d 149, 171 (1st Cir. 1988).

discoverable is an objective one.[32] Stating the proposition affirma-
tively, a plaintiff can recover damages in excess of those stated in the
administrative claim where it can show that unexpected symptoms or
problems developed after the claim was filed,[33] a condition reasonably thought to be temporary proved to be permanent,[34] or a condition was not reasonably discoverable when the claim was filed.[35]
A change in law has been held to constitute an intervening fact for
§ 2675(b) purposes.[36]

Some courts have stretched to reject the government's § 2675(b)
arguments.[37] For example, lack of education and ignorance of the law
regarding lost wages were held to constitute "exceptional factors that
would allow plaintiff to claim an amount greater than that which

---

32. Dickerson v. United States, 280 F.3d 470, 476 (5th Cir. 2002) ("[T]here is an objective test as to whether the plaintiff could have made out its worst-case scenario based on
the basic severity of the injuries that were known.") (citing *Reilly*, 863 F.2d at 172–73); *see*
Michels v. United States, 31 F.3d 686, 689 (8th Cir. 1994); Richardson v. United States,
841 F.2d 993, 999 (9th Cir. 1988).

It has been suggested that a "reasonably foreseeable" test may be easier to meet
than a "worst-case scenario" test. *Compare* Read, *supra* note 26, at 806–14 (discussing
cases), *with Michels*, 31 F.3d at 689 ("We perceive little if any conflict among these cases,
only different facts.").

33. *See* Spivey v. United States, 912 F.2d 80, 86 (4th Cir.1990) (tardive dyskinesia).

34. *See* Cole v. United States, 861 F.2d 1261, 1262 (11th Cir. 1988) (knee injury recognized to be permanent when thrombophlebitis developed).

35. *See* Zurba v. United States, 318 F.3d 736, 742 (7th Cir. 2003) (noting plaintiff
"could not reasonably discover her psychiatric illness until she had suffered the precipitant
events" subsequent to filing her claim).

36. *See* Funston v. United States, 513 F. Supp. 1000, 1007 (M.D. Pa. 1981) (accepting
as new fact Pennsylvania's adoption of total offset rule for calculating future damages).

37. *Compare* Exec. Jet Aviation, Inc. v. United States, 507 F.2d 508, 516 n.4 (6th Cir.
1974) ("[T]here are several cases in which litigants have been permitted to sue the United
States for damages in excess of the amount stated in the administrative claim despite
the prohibition of such suits in 28 U.S.C. § 2675(b).") (citing McCarter v. United States,
373 F. Supp. 1152 (E.D. Tenn. 1973); Little v. United States, 317 F. Supp. 8 (E.D. Pa. 1970);
Rabovsky v. United States, 265 F. Supp. 587 (D. Conn. 1967)); *with* Esquivel-Lachar v.
United States, No. 14-14351-CIV, 2015 WL 8928640, at *4 (S.D. Fla. Dec. 16, 2015). *See
generally* JAYSON & LONGSTRETH, *supra* note 18, § 10.04[7][a] (discussing cases).

was claimed before the agency."[38] This line of reasoning has been criticized as inconsistent with the FTCA's statutory language.[39]

[I]f the exact nature, extent and duration of each recognized disability must be known before § 2675(b) will be given effect, that section will be rendered useless; and the government will be unable to evaluate any claim made against it without the threat that, if it does not settle, its liability may increase substantially.[40]

The safer course for any claimant is to state a sum certain that exceeds the expected value of the claim. An administrative claim that has a low sum certain can be amended at any time before the agency takes final action on it.[41]

C. No Punitive Damages

The FTCA specifically states that "[t]he United States . . . shall not be liable . . . for punitive damages."[42] In its *Molzof* opinion, the Supreme Court held that the meaning of "punitive damages" in § 2674 is a question of federal law.[43] Resolving a dispute among the circuit courts of appeal, the Court held that § 2674 forbids "awards of 'punitive damages,' not 'damages awards that may have a punitive effect.'"[44]

---

38. *See* McCarter v. United States, 373 F. Supp. 1152, 1153 (E.D. Tenn. 1973); *see also* Hilburn v. United States, 789 F. Supp. 338, 342 (D. Haw. 1992) ("The court cannot reconcile the primary goal of the FTCA . . . with a holding that excepts minor children from any and all obligation to fulfill the administrative requirements imposed by the FTCA, especially the 'sum certain' requirement under 28 U.S.C. 2675(b).").

39. *See* Davis v. United States, 244 F. Supp. 2d 878, 880–81 (N.D. Ill. 2002), *aff'd*, 375 F.3d 590 (7th Cir. 2004); Schubach v. United States, 657 F. Supp. 348, 350 n.5 (D. Me. 1987) ("[*McCarter* does not at all square with the specific language of the statute relaxing the limitation upon the amount of a permitted claim and, in the view of this Court, does not give due recognition to the serious purpose of the statutory language in defining the consent of the United States to be sued in tort.").

40. Low v. United States, 795 F.2d 466, 471 (5th Cir. 1986).

41. 28 C.F.R. § 14.2(c). The amendment must "be submitted in writing and signed by the claimant or his authorized agent or legal representative." *Id.* If an amendment is timely filed, the agency has six months "to make a final disposition of the claim as amended and the claimant's option under 28 U.S.C. 2575(a) shall not accrue until six months after the filing of an amendment." 28 C.F.R. § 14.2; *see* McFarlane v. United States, 684 F. Supp. 780, 782 (E.D.N.Y. 1988).

42. 28 U.S.C. § 2674.

43. Molzof v. United States, 502 U.S. 301, 305 (1992).

44. *Id.* at 306.

Accordingly, it stated that the United States is liable for damages which are not "punitive" but "which are for some reason above and beyond ordinary notions of compensation . . . ."[45] It concluded that, "§ 2674 bars the recovery only of what are legally considered 'punitive damages' under traditional common-law principles," and reasoned that the damages in the case before it were "not punitive damages under the common law or the FTCA because their recoverability does not depend upon any proof that the defendant has engaged in intentional or egregious misconduct and their purpose is not to punish."[46]

As interpreted by *Molzof*, § 2674 supports dismissal of any claim plaintiff characterizes as seeking "punitive damages."[47] It also prohibits the award of damages that are enhanced because of the government's intentional or egregious conduct or that are intended to punish.[48] For instance, state laws that enhance wrongful death damages because of aggravating circumstances are punitive within the meaning of § 2674.[49] On the other hand, one court has held that § 2674 does not bar application of "willful and wanton" standards against the United States to disallow a reduction in damages for a plaintiff's comparative negligence.[50]

D. Accounting for Taxes in FTCA Damages

Whether the value of federal income taxes should be deducted from FTCA damage awards turns on both state and federal law. The issue arises because federal tax law excludes from the recipient's gross

---

45. *Id.* at 308.

46. *Id.* at 312.

47. *See* Nurse v. United States, 226 F.3d 996, 1004 (9th Cir. 2000); McEntee v. Henderson, 154 F. Supp. 2d 1286, 1292 (S.D. Ohio 2001).

48. *See Molzof*, 502 U.S. at 312.

49. *See* Beller v. United States, 296 F. Supp. 2d 1277, 1279 (D.N.M. 2003) (citing NMSA 1978, § 41-2–3); Havrum v. United States, 95-4207-CV-C-5, 1998 WL 35223750, at *8 (W.D. Mo. June 19, 1998) ("aggravating circumstances damages in wrongful death cases under Missouri law are punitive in nature"). *But cf.* Munyua v. United States, 03-4538 MMC, 2004 WL 345269, at *2 (N.D. Cal. Feb. 3, 2004) (declining to dismiss count seeking "'treble damages' and a 'civil penalty of $25,000' . . . [for] depriv[ing] the plaintiff of specified rights set forth in the California Civil Code").

50. *See* Brewer v. United States, 864 F. Supp. 741, 747–48 (N.D. Ill. 1994) ("[W]here a plaintiff seeks his full compensatory damages by disallowing an offset which recognizes plaintiff's own comparative fault, Illinois' willful and wanton doctrine may be pleaded in an FTCA lawsuit without violating the strictures of § 2674.").

income money received as non-punitive damages for personal injuries.[51] This means that a damages award in the amount of the lost wages effectively provides compensation that exceeds the plaintiff's out of pocket loss because, unlike wages, it will not be taxed. For example, if a plaintiff's annual salary was $100,000 and she was in a 25% tax bracket, her take-home pay would be $75,000. If a defendant's negligence caused her to miss work for that year, an award or settlement of $100,000 for the lost wages would be tax free and would provide her with $100,000 in after-tax income; that is, $25,000 more than she would have had if she had not been injured. Because this would provide compensation that exceeds the plaintiff's loss, some states reduce personal injury damage awards by the amount of the tax benefit.[52] Other states do not.[53]

---

51. 26 U.S.C. § 104 provides:

Compensation for injuries or sickness,

(a) In general. Except in the case of amounts attributable to (and not in excess of) deductions allowed under section 213 [IRC Sec. 213] (relating to medical, etc., expenses) for any prior taxable year, gross income does not include— . . .

(2) the amount of any damages (other than punitive damages) received (whether by suit or agreement and whether as lump sums or as periodic payments) on account of personal physical injuries or physical sickness . . . .

52. *See, e.g.*, Smith v. Indus. Constructors, Inc., 783 F.2d 1249, 1253 (5th Cir. 1986) ("[D]istrict court's reduction of the decedent's estimated future earnings by the amount of estimated income taxes is perfectly in accord with Mississippi law."); Floyd v. Fruit Indus., 136 A.2d 918, 925–26 (Conn. 1957); Adams v. Deur, 173 N.W.2d 100, 105 (Iowa 1969); Curtis v. Finneran, 417 A.2d 15, 18 (N.J. 1980) ("[P]laintiff's recovery must be calculated on the basis of the deceased's net income after taxes giving due regard to the evidence adduced on the deceased's income tax liability.") (citations and internal quotation marks omitted); N.Y. Est. Powers & Trusts Law § 5-4.3(b) (iii) (McKinney) ("In any such action tried without a jury, the court shall consider the amount of federal, state and local personal income taxes which the court finds, with reasonable certainty, that the decedent would have been obligated by law to pay in determining the sum that would otherwise be available for the support of persons for whom the action is brought."). *See generally* 16 A.L.R. 4th 589 (2009) (collecting cases).

53. . *See, e.g.*, Plant v. Simmons Co., 321 F. Supp. 735, 739 (D. Md. 1970) (applying Maryland law); Hoyal v. Pioneer Sand Co., Inc., 188 P.3d 716, 717 (Colo. 2008) (en banc) ("We hold that evidence of a decedent's future income tax liability should not be considered when calculating net pecuniary loss to a plaintiff in a wrongful death action."); Klawonn v. Mitchell, 475 N.E.2d 857, 859 (Ill. 1985); CSX Transp., Inc. v. Begley, 313 S.W.3d 52, 66 (Ky. 2010) ("Most states, including Kentucky, consider tax implications to be immaterial to the calculation of damages for personal injury."); Hicks v. Jones, 617 S.E.2d 457, 464–65 (W. Va. 2005). *See generally* 16 A.L.R. 4th 589 (2009) (collecting cases).

If a state's damages law normally reduces personal injury awards to reflect income taxes, FTCA awards arising under that state's substantive tort law will similarly deduct the amount of income taxes.[54] Even if the applicable state's damages law does not subtract income taxes from personal injury judgments, there is a question whether federal law compels such a subtraction from FTCA awards. Several arguments have been offered to support this subtraction.[55]

First, it is argued that the purpose of the FTCA is to compensate, and allowing recovery for lost income without reduction for taxes provides a windfall to plaintiffs.[56] As the Supreme Court explained in *Liepelt*, "It is his after-tax income, rather than his gross income before taxes, that provides the only realistic measure of his ability to support his family. It follows inexorably that the wage earner's income tax is a relevant factor in calculating the monetary loss suffered by his dependents when he dies."[57]

Second, some courts coupled this understanding of the FTCA's compensation purpose with § 2674's prohibition of punitive damages to conclude that the FTCA requires deduction of taxes from personal injury awards.[58] Other courts found this argument unpersuasive and inconsistent with § 2674's statutory language requiring

---

54. United States v. English, 521 F.2d 63, 71 (9th Cir. 1975) (applying California law); O'Connor v. United States, 269 F.2d 578, 584–85 (2d Cir. 1959) (applying Oklahoma law); Burton v. United States, 668 F. Supp. 2d 86, 109, 111 (D.D.C. 2009) (applying D.C. law; "federal and state income taxes that would have been paid by Capt. Burton must be deducted"); In re Air Crash Disaster at Charlotte, N.C. on July 2, 1994, 982 F. Supp. 1101, 1112 (D.S.C. 1997) ("[I]n calculating damages under North Carolina law, the court should consider the effect of income taxes.").

55. See Harden v. United States, 688 F.2d 1025, 1029 (5th Cir. 1982); Felder v. United States, 543 F.2d 657, 667 (9th Cir. 1976). See generally Schuler v. United States, 675 F. Supp. 1088, 1094 (W.D. Mich. 1987), rev'd, 868 F.2d 195 (6th Cir. 1989) (finding no liability); JAYSON & LONGSTRETH, supra note 18, at § 10.04[8].

56. See Schuler, 675 F. Supp. at 1094 (citing Trevino v. United States, 804 F.2d 1512 (9th Cir. 1986)); JAYSON & LONGSTRETH, supra note 18, § 10.04[8] (citing Flannery v. United States, 718 F.2d 108 (4th Cir. 1983)).

57. Norfolk & W. Ry. Co. v. Liepelt, 444 U.S. 490, 493–94 (1980) (applying federal law in Federal Employers' Liability Act case).

58. See, e.g., Shaw v. United States, 741 F.2d 1202, 1206 (9th Cir. 1984); Flannery v. United States, 718 F.2d 108, 110 (4th Cir. 1983); Harden v. United States, 688 F.2d 1025, 1029 (5th Cir. 1982).

liability to be measured by state law.[59] In light of the Supreme Court's 1992 *Molzof* opinion[60] the punitive damages leg of this analysis is severely undermined.[61]

Third, one of the reasons for not excluding income tax from tort damages is its potential to confuse juries.[62] Since FTCA cases are tried to the bench, jury confusion cannot be a problem.[63] Accordingly, jury confusion is not a reason to avoid subtracting income tax from compensation awarded for lost wages.[64] A tangential argument not specific to the FTCA is that excluding income tax information is an evidentiary matter and, accordingly, is controlled by federal rather than state law for cases tried in federal courts.[65]

Fourth, because the United States is both the defendant and the taxing authority, it suffers a double loss if federal taxes are not subtracted from FTCA damages, putting it in a categorically different position than other defendants for this issue.[66] A minority view distinguishes between federal taxes (subtracted from FTCA damages) and state taxes (not subtracted).[67]

Some courts have suggested it is more appropriate to subtract taxes from awards to FTCA plaintiffs with higher as opposed to lower incomes.[68] If a subtraction of taxes is otherwise required none will

---

59. *See, e.g.*, Manko v. United States, 830 F.2d 831, 836 (8th Cir. 1987); Kalavity v. United States, 584 F.2d 809, 813 (6th Cir. 1978).

60. *See* discussion *supra* at notes 42–46.

61. *See* Kirchgessner v. United States, 958 F.2d 158, 163 (6th Cir. 1992); Childs v. United States, 923 F. Supp. 1570, 1584 (S.D. Ga. 1996); *see also* Palmer v. United States, 146 F.3d 361, 367 (6th Cir. 1998).

62. *See* McWeeney v. N.Y., New Haven & Hartford R.R. Co., 282 F.2d 34, 37 (2d Cir. 1960).

63. *See supra* Chapter 6.B.

64. *See* Kalavity v. United States, 584 F.2d 809, 812 (6th Cir. 1978); Felder v. United States, 543 F.2d 657, 665 (9th Cir. 1976); Schuler v. United States, 675 F. Supp. 1088, 1094 (W.D. Mich. 1987), *rev'd*, 868 F.2d 195 (6th Cir. 1989).

65. *See* Smith v. Indus. Constrs, Inc., 783 F.2d 1249, 1254 (5th Cir. 1986); *In re* Air Crash Disaster near Chi., 701 F.2d 1189, 1193 (7th Cir. 1983).

66. *See* Flannery v. United States, 718 F.2d 108, 111 (4th Cir. 1983); Felder v. United States, 543 F.2d 657, 670 n.17 (9th Cir. 1976).

67. *See* Burke v. United States, 605 F. Supp. 981, 991 (D. Md. 1985) ("The reasoning behind the federal income tax exception is not applicable to State taxes. State taxes are strictly between the plaintiff and the State.").

68. *See* Kalavity, 584 F.2d at 812; *Felder*, 543 F.2d at 665.

be made if plaintiff's income is so low that he would owe no taxes.[69] Several courts have held that when a reduction for income taxes is appropriate the United States bears the burden of producing evidence to show the expected value of those taxes.[70]

E. No Pre-Judgment Interest

The FTCA provides that "[t]he United States . . . shall not be liable for interest prior to judgment . . . ."[71] The meaning of this language is a question of federal law.[72] Its prohibition of "interest prior to judgment" bars damages for the "advantage to the United States from its possession of the money damages from the time of the injury to the date of judgment or, conversely, the disadvantage or loss to the plaintiff occasioned by the fact that the payment of the damage award occurred . . . years after the injury was suffered."[73] Accordingly, the FTCA bars claims for pre-judgment interest[74] and other claims that directly or indirectly seek compensation for the loss of use of money.[75] For example, it applies to claims for "the present value of amounts lost from . . . death until judgment was rendered,"[76] the loss of earnings on certificates of deposit,[77] and the time value of money.[78]

---

69. *See* Nunsuch v. United States, 221 F. Supp. 2d 1027, 1069 (D. Ariz. 2001) ("Plaintiff would not have earned enough money to owe any federal or state income taxes, and no deductions (or additions for future taxes) need to be made.").

70. *See* Miller v. United States *ex rel.* Dept. of Army, 901 F.2d 894, 897 (10th Cir. 1990) ("The burden is on the defendant to prove the amount to be reduced from future earnings to reflect the effect of income taxes."); Barnes v. United States, 685 F.2d 66, 69 (3d Cir. 1982) ("Assuming *arguendo* that an FTCA award for loss of future earnings must be reduced by projected taxes . . . we conclude that the government failed to meet its burden.").

71. 28 U.S.C. § 2674; *see* Poirier v. United States, 745 F. Supp. 23, 34 (D. Me. 1990).

72. *See* S. Pac. Transp. Co. v. United States, 471 F. Supp. 1186, 1188 (E.D. Cal. 1979).

73. *Id.* at 1197.

74. *See* McDonald v. United States, 555 F. Supp. 935, 972–74 (M.D. Pa. 1983) (rejecting argument that pre-judgment interest bar does not apply to Swine Flu Act case).

75. *See* Preston v. United States, 776 F.2d 754, 760 (7th Cir. 1985); *S. Pac. Transp. Co.*, 471 F. Supp. at 1188.

76. Burton v. United States, 668 F. Supp. 2d 86, 112 (D.D.C. 2009).

77. *See* Marchese v. United States, 781 F. Supp. 241, 247 (S.D.N.Y. 1991) (holding § 2674 bars claim seeking money plaintiffs "could have earned on the principal amounts on their certificates of deposit if the FDIC had not withheld them").

78. *See* Barrett v. United States, 660 F. Supp. 1291, 1319 (S.D.N.Y. 1987).

It also bars the award of interest from the first of multiple judgments in the same case.[79] There is a split of authority as to whether § 2674 prohibits judgments that account for reduced purchasing power.[80]

In *Preston v. United States* the Seventh Circuit held the prejudgment interest bar applied to a claim for the loss of use of grain.[81] Plaintiffs alleged that for years the government had improperly converted grain they had placed in storage.[82] Plaintiffs argued that they should have the value of the loss of their grain over the twelve-year period.[83] The Seventh Circuit affirmed a damage award that compensated plaintiffs only for the value of their converted grain, not the loss of its use:

> In reality, the plaintiffs are seeking an award of prejudgment interest since they would have sold the grain if the CCC had not converted it and since they would have been able to obtain interest on the proceeds from this sale. Compensation for the use of money damages prior to judgment would clearly be an award of prejudgment interest, which is barred by the Federal Tort Claims Act. . . . Although the courts have allowed recovery for loss of use damages for items that can be used for the production of income in the future, the courts have not allowed recovery of an award that represents either an advantage to the United States from its possession of money damages from the time of the injury to the date of the judgment or a disadvantage or loss to the plaintiff occasioned by the fact that payment of the damage award occurred some months or years after the injury was suffered.[84]

---

79. *See* Palmer v. United States, 146 F.3d 361, 366 (6th Cir. 1998); Gross v. United States, 723 F.2d 609, 614 (8th Cir. 1983).

80. *Compare* Lucas v. United States, 807 F.2d 414, 423 (5th Cir. 1986) ("Plaintiffs seek prejudgment interest on the ground that it took the district judge a full year to render judgment. The argument is without merit."), *and Preston*, 776 F.2d at 760, *and* Irving v. United States, 942 F. Supp. 1483, 1513 (D.N.H. 1996), *rev'd on other grounds*, 162 F.3d 154 (1st Cir. 1998) (en banc), *with* McMichael v. United States, 856 F.2d 1026, 1036 (8th Cir. 1988) (allowing evidence of 50% inflation over ten-year period).

81. *Preston*, 776 F.2d at 760.

82. *Id.* at 756–58.

83. *Id.* at 760.

84. *Id.* (citing *S. Pac. Transp. Co.*, 471 F. Supp. at 1197).

CHAPTER 9

Source of Payment, Attorney's Fees, Costs, and Interest

A. Source of Payment

While the source of payment of FTCA judgments and settlements is normally noncontroversial, the statutory basis for such payments may have consequences in particular cases or settlement negotiations. The significant point is that agency funds are not used to pay FTCA judgments or FTCA settlements in excess of $2,500.[1]

The Appropriations Clause of the United States Constitution[2] requires a specific funding source for any government payment, including settlements and court-ordered judgments.[3] It is black letter law that agency appropriations cannot be used to pay judgments against the United States or its agencies, absent specific authorizing legislation.[4] Such legislation could be an appropriation for a

---

1. 28 U.S.C. § 2672 (2012); 3 U.S. Gen. Accounting Office, Office of the Gen. Counsel, GAO-08-078SP, Principles of Federal Appropriations Law §§ 14–30 to –44 (3d ed. 2008), *available at* http://www.gao.gov/special.pubs/d08978sp.pdf. The rare exceptions include nonappropriated fund instrumentalities, *id.* at 15–266, community health centers, 42 U.S.C. § 233(k), and the U.S. Postal Service, 39 U.S.C. § 409(h). 3 U.S. Gen. Accounting Office, Office of the Gen. Counsel, GAO/OGC-94-33, Principles of Federal Appropriations Law §§ 14–34 to –37 (2d ed. 1994), *available at* http://www.gao.gov/special.pubs/og94033.pdf.
2. U.S. Const. art. I, § 9, cl. 7.
3. U.S. Gov't Accountability Office, GAO-08-978SP, Principles of Federal Appropriations Law §§ 14–31 to –32 (3d ed. 2008) [hereinafter GAO-08-978SP] (citing Office of Pers. Mgmt. v. Richmond, 496 U.S. 414, 424–26 (1990)), *available at* http://www.gao.gov/special.pubs/d08978sp.pdf.
4. *Id.* §§ 14–30 to –44. *But see* 28 U.S.C. § 2672 (2006) (settlements for less than $2,500).

particular settlement or judgment, a general appropriation for categories of settlements or judgments, or a statute that authorizes payments from a pre-existing appropriation.[5]

When it was enacted in 1946, the FTCA authorized the use of agency appropriations to pay settlements of up to $1,000,[6] later amended to $2,500.[7] Judgments and settlements for larger amounts could not be paid until Congress specifically appropriated money to pay them.[8] In 1956 Congress created the Judgment Fund, a permanent, indefinite appropriation for the payment of judgments of up to $100,000.[9] Under the new procedure, any FTCA judgment for that amount or less was paid automatically.[10] In 1961 use of the Judgment Fund was expanded to include settlements of up to $100,000.[11] In 1977 Congress opened the Judgment Fund to pay, *inter alia*, any

---

5. *See* GAO-08-978SP §§ 14-31 to –32.

6. The Legislative Reorganization Act of 1946, Pub. L. No. 79-601, 60 Stat, 812, 843, provides in part:

> SEC. 4.03 CLAIMS OF $1,000 OR LESS
>
> * * *
>
> (c) Any award made to any claimant pursuant to this section, and any award, compromise, or settlement of any claim cognizable under this title made by the Attorney General pursuant to section 413, shall be paid by the head of the Federal agency concerned out of appropriations that may be made therefor, which appropriations are hereby authorized.

7. An Act to amend title 28 of the United States Code to increase the limit for administrative settlement of claims against the United States under the tort claims procedure to $2,500, 86 Pub. L. No. 238; 73 Stat. 471 (1959).

8. *See* GAO-08-978SP §§ 14–31.

9. Supplemental Appropriation Act of 1957, Pub. L. No. 84-814, § 1302, 70 Stat. 678, 694–95 (1956) (now codified at 31 U.S.C. § 1304 (2006)). The statute provided, *inter alia*:

> There are appropriated, out of any money in the Treasury not otherwise appropriated, and out of the postal revenues, respectively, such sums as may hereafter be necessary for the payment, not otherwise provide for, as certified by the Comptroller General, of judgments (not in excess of $100,000 in any one case) rendered by the district courts and the Court of Claims against the United States which have become final together with such interest and costs as may be specified in such judgments or otherwise authorized by law. . . .

Id.

10. *Id.*

11. An Act to simplify the payment of certain miscellaneous judgments and the payment of certain compromise settlements, Pub. L. No. 87-187, § 2, 75 Stat. 415, 416, (1961).

FTCA judgment regardless of amount, and any FTCA settlement for more than $2,500.[12]

B. Attorney's Fees

The FTCA contemplates that attorney's fees will be paid from the judgment or settlement.[13] It limits the amount of such fees to no more than twenty percent of any administrative settlement or twenty-five percent of any judgment or settlement entered after suit is filed.[14] Attorney's fees for structured settlements are calculated as a percentage of the total amount expended by the government to reach the settlement, including money paid to purchase annuities, fund trusts, and make cash payments to claimants or plaintiffs.[15]

The FTCA did not waive sovereign immunity to allow recovery of attorney's fees incurred in FTCA litigation.[16] Accordingly, attorney's fees incurred in the litigation cannot be included as an element of plaintiff's FTCA damages.[17] Some authority holds that attorney's fees may be recovered as damages under the FTCA if they were incurred because of a government tort.[18] The Equal Access to Justice Act (EAJA) includes provisions authorizing the award of attorney's fees against

---

12. *See* Supplemental Appropriations Act of 1977, Pub. L. No. 95-26, ch. 14, 91 Stat. 61, 96–97 (1977).

13. *See* Joe v. United States, 772 F.2d 1535, 1537 (11th Cir. 1985); Dockery v. United States, 663 F. Supp. 2d 111, 126 (N.D.N.Y. 2009) (holding that "attorney's fees should come out of the judgment awarded pursuant to the bench trial, and the court will not assess attorney fees in this order.").

14. 28 U.S.C. § 2678.

15. *See* Wyatt v. United States, 783 F.2d 45, 49–50 (6th Cir. 1986); Godwin v. Schram, 731 F.2d 153,157–58 (3d Cir. 1984); *see also* LESTER S. JAYSON & ROBERT C. LONGSTRETH, HANDLING FEDERAL TORT CLAIMS § 10-01 (2018) (discussing cases).

16. *See* Anderson v. United States, 127 F.3d 1190, 1191 (9th Cir. 1997) ("The FTCA does not contain an express waiver of sovereign immunity for attorneys' fees and expenses.").

17. *See* Johnson v. United States, 780 F.2d 902, 910 (11th Cir. 1986) ("The district court . . . had no authority to separately award attorney's fees against the United States and should not have included in its damage judgment any amount 'for the payment of attorney's fees.'").

18. *See* Tri-State Hosp. Supply Corp. v. United States, 341 F.3d 571, 572 (D.C. Cir. 2003) ("We . . . hold that attorney's fees *qua* damages are recoverable against the United States for abuse of process and malicious prosecution if 'the law of the place' where the tort occurred so provides.").

the United States in some circumstances,[19] but explicitly excludes them in "cases sounding in tort."[20]

C. Costs

Costs of litigation (other than attorney's fees) are available from the United States in FTCA litigation in the same manner as they are available against any other defendant.[21] They may include fees for witnesses, transcripts, necessary copying, and compensation for interpreters.[22] Fees for expert witnesses' are not taxable costs in FTCA litigation.[23]

D. Interest

Absent express statutory authority interest cannot be awarded against the United States.[24] The FTCA explicitly bars recovery for "interest prior to judgment."[25] Very specific procedures and the interaction of two statutes limit the amount and availability of post-judgment interest. The provisions of 28 U.S.C. § 1961(a) generally make interest payable on "any money judgment in a civil case recovered in a district court . . . at a rate equal to the weekly average 1-year constant maturity Treasury yield, as published by the Board of Governors of

---

19. *See* 28 U.S.C. § 2412.

20. *See* 28 U.S.C. § 2412(b); *In re* Turner, 14 F.3d 637, 640 (D.C. Cir. 1994) (holding EAJA's "statutory exception . . . for 'cases sounding in tort' forecloses an award of attorney's fees" in federal employee's suit under FTCA to be certified as acting within scope of employment); Campbell v. United States, 835 F.2d 193, 196 (9th Cir. 1987); Epling v. United States, 958 F. Supp. 312, 316 (W.D. Ky. 1997). *But c.f.* Tri-State Hosp. Supply Corp. v. United States, 341 F.3d at 581 (holding that EAJA did not preclude recovery of attorney's fees as an element of damages).

21. *See* 28 U.S.C § 2412(a); JAYSON & LONGSTRETH, *supra* note 15, at § 16-10[2].

22. *See* 28 U.S.C § 1920.

23. *See* JAYSON & LONGSTRETH, *supra* note 15, at § 16-10[2] (citing United States v. Kolesar, 313 F.2d 835 (5th Cir. 1963); Romero v. United States, 865 F. Supp. 585, 594–95 (E.D. Mo. 1994)). *See generally* Crawford Fitting Co. v. J.T. Gibbons, Inc., 482 U.S. 437, 445 (1987) ("absent explicit statutory or contractual authorization for the taxation of the expenses of a litigant's witness as costs, federal courts are bound by the limitations set out in 28 U.S.C. § 1821 and § 1920.").

24. *See* Library of Congress v. Shaw, 478 U.S. 310, 311 (1986); Starns v. United States, 923 F.2d 34, 38 (4th Cir. 1991) (FTCA suit).

25. 28 U.S.C. § 2674.

the Federal Reserve System, for the calendar week preceding the date of the judgment."[26] The next subsection specifically notes that "Interest shall be computed daily to the date of payment except as provided in . . . section 1304(b) of title 31, and shall be compounded annually."[27] Section 1304(b)(1) of title 31 provides:

(b) (1) Interest may be paid from the appropriation made by this section—

(A) on a judgment of a district court, only when the judgment becomes final after review on appeal or petition by the United States Government, and then only from the date of filing of the transcript of the judgment with the Secretary of the Treasury through the day before the date of the mandate of affirmance . . . .

Accordingly, interest on an FTCA judgment can be paid only if there is an appeal by the United States[28] and the transcript of the judgment was filed with the Secretary of the Treasury.[29] It is the plaintiff's burden to file the transcript with the Secretary of the Treasury.[30] If all the

---

26. 28 U.S.C. § 1961(a).

27. 28 U.S.C. § 1961(b).

28. *See* MacDonald v. United States, 825 F. Supp. 683, 686 (M.D. Pa. 1993) ("Section 1304 permits a prevailing FTCA plaintiff to recover interest only for the period during which the judgment is on appeal."), *aff'd*, 22 F.3d 302 (3d Cir. 1994).

29. *See* Moyer v. United States, 612 F. Supp. 239, 241 (D. Nev. 1985); Jayson & Long-streth, *supra* note 15, at § 16-10[1] (discussing cases).

30. *See* Rooney v. United States, 694 F.2d 582, 583 (9th Cir. 1982); MacDonald v. United States, 825 F. Supp. 683, 686 (M.D. Pa. 1993), *aff'd*, 22 F.3d 302 (3d Cir. 1994). The pertinent regulation, 31 C.F.R. § 256.32, provides:

Sec. 256.32 What documentation must be submitted to the Judgment Fund Branch to preserve the right to seek interest under 31 U.S.C. 1304(b) in a case where the government has taken an appeal?

31 U.S.C. 1304(b) specifies that a "transcript of the judgment" must be filed with the Secretary of the Treasury. This means that a copy of the judgment must be filed with the Judgment Fund Branch for interest to accrue on a judgment of a federal district court, the Court of Appeals for the Federal Circuit, or the United States Court of Federal Claims. By practice, the successful plaintiff files a copy of the judgment. Whoever submits the judgment should include a cover letter explaining that it is being submitted to preserve interest rights under 31 U.S.C. 1304. A copy of the judgment and cover letter must be sent to the Financial Management Service, Judgment Fund Branch, at the address indicated on the Judgment Fund Web site at http://www.fms.treas.gov/judgefund.

Contact information for the Financial Management Service, Judgment Fund Branch and a sample letter are provided in Appendix E.

procedures of § 1304(b)(1) are complied with, interest will be paid at "weekly average 1-year constant maturity Treasury yield"[31] compounded annually[32] from the date the transcript is filed with Treasury until the day before the mandate is issued.[33]

---

31. 28 U.S.C. § 1961(a).

32. 28 U.S.C. § 1961(b).

33. 31 U.S.C. § 1304(b)(1)(A); see Dickerson v. United States, 280 F.3d 470, 478–79 (5th Cir. 2002); Desart v. United States, 947 F.2d 871, 872 (9th Cir. 1991).

CHAPTER 10

Settlement

The FTCA administrative claims process does work. Settlement of valid cases is the key goal of the FTCA.[1] Most administrative claims are resolved at the agency level and do not proceed to litigation.[2] Moreover, it is reported that over sixty percent of litigated FTCA cases end in settlement.[3]

In many ways, negotiating a settlement for a run-of-the-mill tort claim under the FTCA is similar to negotiating such a claim with a private party or insurance company. Both sides will weigh the likelihood of a finding of liability and the likely range of damages to arrive at an expected value for the claim. As in any tort negotiation, other considerations will color the analysis. Are there problems of proof for plaintiff's case in chief or for applicable affirmative defenses? If expert witnesses are involved, are they credible, prepared, and likely to be effective? Is the plaintiff particularly sympathetic, troubled, or in dire need of prompt resolution? If trial date is approaching, are the parties equally prepared?

FTCA settlement negotiations differ from their private counterparts in important ways. Any FTCA settlement will have to be approved by an officer with the appropriate level of authority after consultation. There is more certainty about the likely range of damages because of specific provisions of the FTCA, and no limit on the ability of the government to pay large judgments.[4] Federal agencies

---

1. *See* Chapter 2.
2. Lester S. Jayson & Robert C. Longstreth, Handling Federal Tort Claims § 17.01 (2018); Jeffrey Axelrad, *Federal Tort Claims Act Administrative Claims: Better Than Third Party ADR for Resolving Federal Tort Claims*, 52 Admin. L. Rev. 1331, 1342–45 (2000).
3. *See* Jayson & Longstreth, *supra* note 2, at § 15.02.
4. *See* Chapter 8.

and federal employee tortfeasors do not have control over settlements as private defendants do. Finally, the government takes the long view in settlement negotiations. It has a long-term interest in fostering effective procedures for settlement, developing favorable jurisprudence, and protecting the public fisc.

All federal agencies have authority to negotiate settlements and to enter settlements of up to $25,000.[5] For larger settlements and cases in litigation, the FTCA vests the government's settlement authority in the Attorney General and allows him to delegate that responsibility.[6] The Attorney General has delegated greater authority to some agencies that handle numerous administrative claims[7] and to officers within the Department of Justice.[8]

A proposed settlement of an FTCA administrative claim will be reviewed by several people. Any agency settlement for more than $2,500 must be approved under established agency procedures and only "after review by a legal officer of the agency."[9] Any settlement negotiated by the agency for an amount over $25,000 (or the agency's delegated settlement authority) will not be valid until it is approved in writing by the Department of Justice.[10] The Attorney General has delegated several levels of authority to approve administrative settlements to Department of Justice officers.[11] The Deputy Attorney General and the Associate Attorney General have authority to approve settlements that exceed $2,000,000.[12] Assistant Attorneys General have authority to approve administrative settlements of up to $2,000,000.[13] Branch Directors have such authority for administrative settlements of up to $1,000,000.[14] The same levels of authority

---

5. *See* 28 U.S.C. § 2672 (2012); 28 C.F.R. § 14.6(c) (2017).

6. *See* 28 U.S.C. § 2672; *see also* 28 U.S.C. § 2677.

7. *See* 28 C.F.R. Part 14, Appendix to Part 14 (included in Appendix C).

8. *See* 28 C.F.R. Part 0, Subpart Y.

9. *See* 28 C.F.R. § 14.5.

10. *See* 28 C.F.R. § 14.5(c).

11. *See* 28 C.F.R. Part 0, Subpart Y. The officers' authority is limited in circumstances that raise particular policy issues. *See, e.g.*, 28 C.F.R § 0.160(d); 28 C.F.R Part 0, Subpart Y, Appendix [Directive No. 1-10] § 1(e).

12. *See* 28 C.F.R. § 0.161(b).

13. *See* 28 C.F.R. § 0.160(a)(2).

14. *See* 28 C.F.R. Part 0, Subpart Y, Appendix [Directive No. 1-10] § 1(b)(1)(ii).

apply to settlement of FTCA cases in litigation, with the addition that United States Attorneys have authority of up to $1,000,000,[15] which they may re-delegate to supervising Assistant United States Attorneys.[16]

Whenever a proposed settlement is approved, a detailed memorandum explaining the settlement must be placed in the file.[17] In practice, that memorandum will be written for the officer with authority and reviewed by each officer with lesser authority.[18] For example, the memorandum supporting a proposed administrative settlement for $1,900,000 would be written by a Civil Division attorney who would attach to it the agency's detailed analysis of the settlement. That memorandum would then be reviewed by the Branch Director who, if satisfied, would forward it to the Assistant Attorney General for approval. The Assistant Attorney General would then decide whether to approve the settlement. The same process would apply if the proposed settlement involved an FTCA case in litigation. This procedure reflects the measured and deliberate decision-making process.

Money plays a different dynamic in FTCA settlements than in private negotiations. Although, as a general matter, FTCA damages are determined under state law, the Act imposes several strong limits.[19] Plaintiffs cannot recover punitive damages,[20] pre-judgment interest,[21] or an amount larger than that stated in the administrative claim.[22] On the other hand, given the government's very deep pockets, plaintiffs can be assured of recovering from the Judgment Fund the complete amount of any FTCA final award.[23]

Because the Judgment Fund pays all litigative settlements and all administrative settlements in excess of $2,500, federal agencies have

15. *Id.*
16. *See* 28 C.F.R. Part 0, Subpart Y, Appendix [Directive No. 1-10] § 1(d).
17. *See, e.g.*, 28 C.F.R. Part 0, Subpart Y, Appendix [Directive No. 1-10] § 2(a).
18. *See, e.g.*, 28 C.F.R. § 0.161(a).
19. *See* Chapter 8.
20. 28 U.S.C. § 2674.
21. *Id.*
22. 28 U.S.C. § 2675(b). The amount can be raised on a showing of "newly discovered evidence" or "intervening facts." *Id.*
23. *See* 31 U.S.C. § 1304; *supra* Chapter 9.A.

no financial stake in the outcome of a typical FTCA claim. Accordingly, federal agencies have less control and institutional interest in the size of FTCA settlements than do typical defendants. Indeed, the Department of Justice has authority to refuse to approve a settlement the agency strongly recommends[24] and to accept a settlement the agency opposes.[25]

The Department of Justice has its own concerns regarding settlements. It has a strong interest in the orderly functioning of the FTCA's administrative claim system.[26] It wants to settle cases, but in a manner that protects the public fisc from exploitation. If a case is clearly barred by some provision of the FTCA, the Department of Justice will not settle. It will listen to agency views, but will not settle an FTCA case to further an agency's programmatic or political concerns. Such settlements would usurp Congress's authority under the Appropriations Clause.[27]

The Department of Justice also wants to develop FTCA jurisprudence and may decline to settle a case that provides a good vehicle for developing precedent. The Department recognizes that any settlement will influence other cases. Accordingly, it has no interest in nuisance settlements, believing that settling one nuisance claim will lead to many others. The centralized system for reviewing settlements allows the Department to manage these concerns.[28]

From a practitioner's viewpoint, some strategies that work in negotiations with private parties will be relatively useless in the FTCA context. Arguments that a settlement will allow an agency to avoid litigation or discovery that might cause it disruption, expense, public embarrassment, or bad publicity will fall on deaf ears because the FTCA was not enacted to protect agencies from those things and

---

24. *See* 28 U.S.C. § 2672; 28 C.F.R. 0.162 ("Offers which may be rejected by Assistant Attorneys General"); 28 C.F.R. Part 0, Subpart Y, Appendix [Directive No. 1-10] § 1(b)(1)(iii) (granting Branch Directors and United States Attorneys authority to "[r]eject any offers.").

25. *See* 28 U.S.C. §§ 2672, 2677; 28 C.F.R. Part 0, Subpart Y, Appendix [Directive No. 1-10] § 1(e)(3) (establishing procedure for review of decision to settle over agency objection).

26. *See generally* McNeil v. United States, 508 U.S. 106, 112–13 (1993).

27. *See* discussion at page 79, *supra*.

28. *See, e.g., In re* Stone, 986 F.2d 898, 903 (5th Cir. 1993).

because the Judgment Fund (the source of payment) cannot properly be used for such purposes.[29] Accordingly, the Department of Justice will not factor those considerations into its analysis of a settlement. The Department of Justice takes its role as guardian of the Judgment Fund very seriously.

Appeals based on the special needs, good character, or horrible suffering of the claimant, to the extent such appeals exceed what a court might consider at trial, will have little impact. The Department of Justice seeks to treat all claimants equally, even those of poor character and without special needs. It will consider each claimant's case on its individual legal and factual merits.

Coming to Washington to meet with Torts Branch attorneys is not likely to expedite a settlement. Given the hierarchy of authority for approval of settlements, the measured, memo-reliant procedure for recommending a settlement approval, and the lack of first-hand knowledge about the case on the part of the Torts Branch attorneys, such a meeting will likely be perfunctory. If, on the other hand, Torts Branch attorneys have primary responsibility for the defense of the case, such a meeting might be productive.

Demands to have the person with ultimate settlement authority present at settlement negotiations will be strongly resisted.[30] For the reasons just noted, such attendance is perceived as a waste of the person with authority's time, particularly if that person is an important member of the Executive Branch with multiple responsibilities such as an Assistant Attorney General, the Associate Attorney General, or the Deputy Attorney General. The United States is in a different position than other litigants "both because of the geographic breadth of government litigation and also, most importantly, because of the nature of the issues the government litigates . . . . [T]he government is a party to a far greater number of cases . . . than even the most litigious private entity . . . ."[31] Court-ordered attendance by the person with settlement authority would be disruptive of the government's

---

29. *See, e.g.*, 31 U.S.C. § 1304.
30. *See In re* Stone, 986 F.2d at 900–01, 904–05.
31. United States v. Mendoza, 464 U.S. 154, 159 (1984).

other business and is unlikely to expedite resolution of the settlement because, *inter alia,* even after a thorough briefing that person will lack detailed firsthand knowledge of the case.

The best way to approach FTCA settlement negotiations with the government is to thoroughly prepare on the factual and legal issues, take a realistic position as to the value of the claim, and negotiate with an understanding of the bureaucratic steps that will be followed before a settlement can be finalized. Often, it will be best for the claimant to make an opening offer. Expect and accept a response that the government's negotiator will "recommend" a particular figure to his superior. The government negotiator will not seek formal approval of a settlement until the claimant has agreed to it and there is a completed agreement for the person with authority to approve.

APPENDIX A

Federal Tort Claims Act

1. 28 U.S.C. § 1346 United States as defendant [Jurisdiction]

* * *

(b)(1) Subject to the provisions of chapter 171 of this title, the district courts, together with the United States District Court for the District of the Canal Zone and the District Court of the Virgin Islands, shall have exclusive jurisdiction of civil actions on claims against the United States, for money damages, accruing on and after January 1, 1945, for injury or loss of property, or personal injury or death caused by the negligent or wrongful act or omission of any employee of the Government while acting within the scope of his office or employment, under circumstances where the United States, if a private person, would be liable to the claimant in accordance with the law of the place where the act or omission occurred.

(2) No person convicted of a felony who is incarcerated while awaiting sentencing or while serving a sentence may bring a civil action against the United States or an agency, officer, or employee of the Government, for mental or emotional injury suffered while in custody without a prior showing of physical injury or the commission of a sexual act (as defined in section 2246 of title 18).

2. 28 U.S.C. § 1402. United States as defendant [Venue]

* * *

(b) Any civil action on a tort claim against the United States under subsection (b) of section 1346 of this title may be prosecuted only in the judicial district where the plaintiff resides or wherein the act or omission complained of occurred.

3. 28 U.S.C. § 2401. Time for commencing action against United States

* * *

(b) A tort claim against the United States shall be forever barred unless it is presented in writing to the appropriate Federal agency within two years after such claim accrues or unless action is begun within six months after the date of mailing, by certified or registered mail, of notice of final denial of the claim by the agency to which it was presented.

4. 28 U.S.C. § 2402. Jury trial in actions against United States

Subject to chapter 179 of this title, any action against the United States under section 1346 shall be tried by the court without a jury, except that any action against the United States under section 1346(a)(1) shall, at the request of either party to such action, be tried by the court with a jury.

5. 28 U.S.C. § 2671, et seq. Tort claims procedures

28 U.S.C. § 2671. Definitions

As used in this chapter and sections 1346(b) and 2401(b) of this title, the term "Federal agency" includes the executive departments, the judicial and legislative branches, the military departments, independent establishments of the United States, and corporations primarily acting as instrumentalities or agencies of the United States, but does not include any contractor with the United States.

"Employee of the government" includes

(1) officers or employees of any Federal agency, members of the military or naval forces of the United States, members of the National Guard while engaged in training or duty under section 115, 316, 502, 503, 504, or 505 of title 32, and persons acting on behalf of a Federal agency in an official capacity, temporarily or permanently in the service of the United States, whether with or without compensation, and

(2) any officer or employee of a Federal public defender organization, except when such officer or employee performs professional services in the course of providing representation under section 3006A of title 18.

"Acting within the scope of his office or employment," in the case of a member of the military or naval forces of the United States or a member of the National Guard as defined in section 101(3) of title 32, means acting in the line of duty.

28 U.S.C. § 2672. Administrative adjustment of claims

The head of each Federal agency or his designee, in accordance with regulations prescribed by the Attorney General, may consider, ascertain, adjust, determine, compromise, and settle any claim for money damages against the United States for injury or loss of property or personal injury or death caused by the negligent or wrongful act or omission of any employee of the agency while acting within the scope of his office or employment, under circumstances where the United States, if a private person, would be liable to the claimant in accordance with the law of the place where the act or omission occurred: Provided, that any award, compromise, or settlement in excess of $25,000 shall be effected only with the prior written approval of the Attorney General or his designee. Notwithstanding the proviso contained in the preceding sentence, any award, compromise, or settlement may be effected without the prior written approval of the Attorney General or his or her designee, to the extent that the Attorney General delegates to the head of the agency the authority to make such award, compromise, or settlement. Such delegations may not exceed the authority delegated by the Attorney General to the United States attorneys to settle claims for money damages against the United States. Each Federal agency may use arbitration, or other alternative means of dispute resolution under the provisions of subchapter IV of chapter 5 of title 5, to settle any tort claim against the United States, to the extent of the agency's authority to award, compromise, or settle such claim without the prior written approval of the Attorney General or his or her designee.

Subject to the provisions of this title relating to civil actions on tort claims against the United States, any such award, compromise, settlement, or determination shall be final and conclusive on all officers of the Government, except when procured by means of fraud. Any award, compromise, or settlement in an amount of $2,500 or less made pursuant to this section shall be paid by the head of the Federal agency concerned out of appropriations available to that agency. Payment of any award, compromise, or settlement in an amount in excess of $2,500 made pursuant to this section or made by the Attorney General in any amount pursuant to section 2677 of this title shall be paid in a manner similar to judgments and compromises in like causes and appropriations or funds available for the payment of such judgments and compromises are hereby made available for the payment of awards, compromises, or settlements under this chapter.

The acceptance by the claimant of any such award, compromise, or settlement shall be final and conclusive on the claimant, and shall constitute a complete release of any claim against the United States and against the employee of the government whose act or omission gave rise to the claim, by reason of the same subject matter.

28 U.S.C. § 2673. [Repealed.]

28 U.S.C. § 2674. Liability of United States

The United States shall be liable, respecting the provisions of this title relating to tort claims, in the same manner and to the same extent as a private individual under like circumstances, but shall not be liable for interest prior to judgment or for punitive damages.

If, however, in any case wherein death was caused, the law of the place where the act or omission complained of occurred provides, or has been construed to provide, for damages only punitive in nature, the United States shall be liable for actual or compensatory damages, measured by the pecuniary injuries resulting from such death to the persons respectively, for whose benefit the action was brought, in lieu thereof.

With respect to any claim under this chapter, the United States shall be entitled to assert any defense based upon judicial or legislative immunity which otherwise would have been available to the employee of the United States whose act or omission gave rise to the claim, as well as any other defenses to which the United States is entitled.

With respect to any claim to which this section applies, the Tennessee Valley Authority shall be entitled to assert any defense which otherwise would have been available to the employee based upon judicial or legislative immunity, which otherwise would have been available to the employee of the Tennessee Valley Authority whose act or omission gave rise to the claim as well as any other defenses to which the Tennessee Valley Authority is entitled under this chapter.

28 U.S.C. § 2675. Disposition by Federal agency as prerequisite; evidence

(a) An action shall not be instituted upon a claim against the United States for money damages for injury or loss of property or personal injury or death caused by the negligent or wrongful act or omission of any employee of the Government while acting within the scope of his office or employment, unless the claimant shall have first presented the claim to the appropriate Federal agency and his claim shall have been finally denied by the agency in writing and sent by certified or registered mail. The failure of an agency to make final disposition of a claim within six months after it is filed shall, at the option of the claimant any time thereafter, be deemed a final denial of the claim for purposes of this section. The provisions of this subsection shall not apply to such claims as may be asserted under the Federal Rules of Civil Procedure by third party complaint, cross-claim, or counterclaim.

(b) Action under this section shall not be instituted for any sum in excess of the amount of the claim presented to the Federal agency, except where the increased amount is based upon newly discovered evidence not reasonably discoverable at the time of presenting the claim to the Federal agency, or upon allegation and proof of intervening facts, relating to the amount of the claim.

(c) Disposition of any claim by the Attorney General or other head of a Federal agency shall not be competent evidence of liability or amount of damages.

28 U.S.C. § 2676. Judgment as bar

The judgment in an action under section 1346(b) of this title shall constitute a complete bar to any action by the claimant, by reason of the same subject matter, against the employee of the government whose act or omission gave rise to the claim.

28 U.S.C. § 2677. Compromise

The Attorney General or his designee may arbitrate, compromise, or settle any claim cognizable under section 1346(b) of this title, after the commencement of an action thereon.

28 U.S.C. § 2678. Attorney fees; penalty

No attorney shall charge, demand, receive, or collect for services rendered, fees in excess of 25 per centum of any judgment rendered pursuant to section 1346(b) of this title or any settlement made pursuant to section 2677 of this title, or in excess of 20 per centum of any award, compromise, or settlement made pursuant to section 2672 of this title.

Any attorney who charges, demands, receives, or collects for services rendered in connection with such claim any amount in excess of that allowed under this section, if recovery be had, shall be fined not more than $2,000 or imprisoned not more than one year, or both.

28 U.S.C. § 2679. Exclusiveness of remedy

(a) The authority of any Federal agency to sue and be sued in its own name shall not be construed to authorize suits against such Federal agency on claims which are cognizable under section 1346(b) of this title, and the remedies provided by this title in such cases shall be exclusive.

(b) (1) The remedy against the United States provided by sections 1346(b) and 2672 of this title for injury or loss of property, or personal injury or death arising or resulting from the negligent or wrongful act or omission of any employee of the Government while acting within the scope of his office or employment is exclusive of any other civil action or proceeding for money damages by reason of the same subject matter against the employee whose act or omission gave rise to the claim or against the estate of such employee. Any other civil action or proceeding for money damages arising out of or relating to the same subject matter against the employee or the employee's estate is precluded without regard to when the act or omission occurred.

(2) Paragraph (1) does not extend or apply to a civil action against an employee of the Government—

(A) which is brought for a violation of the Constitution of the United States, or

(B) which is brought for a violation of a statute of the United States under which such action against an individual is otherwise authorized.

(c) The Attorney General shall defend any civil action or proceeding brought in any court against any employee of the Government or his estate for any such damage or injury. The employee against whom such civil action or proceedings is brought shall deliver within such time after date of service or knowledge of service as determined by the Attorney General, all process served upon him or an attested true copy thereof to his immediate superior or to whomever was designated by the head of his department to receive such papers and such person shall promptly furnish copies of the pleadings and process therein to the United States attorney for the district embracing the place wherein the proceeding is brought, to the Attorney General, and to the head of his employing Federal agency.

(d) (1) Upon certification by the Attorney General that the defendant employee was acting within the scope of his office or employment at the time of the incident out of which the claim arose, any civil action or proceeding commenced upon such claim in a United States district court shall be deemed an action against the United States under the provisions of this title and all references thereto, and the United States shall be substituted as the party defendant.

(2) Upon certification by the Attorney General that the defendant employee was acting within the scope of his office or employment at the time of the incident out of which the claim arose, any civil action or proceeding commenced upon such claim in a State court shall be removed without bond at any time before trial by the Attorney General to the district court of the United States for the district and division embracing the place in which the action or proceeding is pending. Such action or proceeding shall be deemed to be an action or proceeding brought against the United States under the provisions of this title and all references thereto, and the United States shall be substituted as the party defendant. This certification of the Attorney General shall conclusively establish scope of office, or employment for purposes of removal.

(3) In the event that the Attorney General has refused to certify scope of office or employment under this section, the employee may at any time before trial petition the court to find and certify that the employee was acting within the scope of his office or employment. Upon such certification by the court, such action or proceeding shall be deemed to be an action or proceeding brought against the United States under the provisions of this title and all references thereto, and the United States shall be substituted as the party defendant. A copy of the petition shall be served upon the United States in accordance with the provisions of Rule 4(d)(4) of the Federal Rules of Civil Procedure. In the event the petition is filed in a civil action or proceeding pending in a State court, the action or proceeding may be removed without

bond by the Attorney General to the district court of the United States for the district and division embracing the place in which it is pending. If, in considering the petition, the district court determines that the employee was not acting within the scope of his office or employment, the action or proceeding shall be remanded to the State court.

(4) Upon certification, any action or proceeding subject to paragraph (1), (2), or (3) shall proceed in the same manner as any action against the United States filed pursuant to section 1346(b) of this title and shall be subject to the limitations and exceptions applicable to those actions.

(5) Whenever an action or proceeding in which the United States is substituted as the party defendant under this subsection is dismissed for failure first to present a claim pursuant to section 2675(a) of this title, such a claim shall be deemed to be timely presented under section 2401(b) of this title if—

(A) the claim would have been timely had it been filed on the date the underlying civil action was commenced, and

(B) the claim is presented to the appropriate Federal agency within 60 days after dismissal of the civil actions.

(e) The Attorney General may compromise or settle any claim asserted in such civil action or proceeding in the manner provided in section 2677, and with the same effect.

28 U.S.C. § 2680. Exceptions

The provisions of this chapter and section 1346(b) of this title shall not apply to—

(a) Any claim based upon an act or omission of an employee of the Government, exercising due care, in the execution of a statute or regulation, whether or not such statute or regulation be valid, or based upon the exercise or performance or the failure to exercise or perform a discretionary function or duty on the part of a Federal agency or an employee of the Government, whether or not the discretion involved be abused.

(b) Any claim arising out of the loss, miscarriage, or negligent transmission of letters or postal matter.

(c) Any claim arising in respect of the assessment or collection of any tax or customs duty, or the detention of any goods, merchandise, or other property by any officer of customs or excise or any other law enforcement officer, except that the provisions of this chapter and section 1346(b) of this title apply to any claim based on injury or loss of goods, merchandise, or other property, while in the possession of any officer or customs or excise or any other law enforcement officer, if—

(1) the property was seized for the purpose of forfeiture under any provision of Federal law providing for the forfeiture of property other than as a sentence imposed upon conviction of a criminal offense;

(2) the interest of the claimant was not forfeited;

(3) the interest of the claimant was not remitted or mitigated (if the property was subject to forfeiture); and

(4) the claimant was not convicted of a crime for which interest of the claimant in the property was subject to forfeiture under a Federal criminal forfeiture law.

(d) Any claim for which a remedy is provided by chapter 309 or 311 of Title 46 [Admiralty Act and the Public Vessels Act], relating to claims or suits in admiralty against the United States.

(e) Any claim arising out of an act or omission of any employee of the Government in administering the provisions of sections 1-31 of Title 50, Appendix [Trading with the Enemy Act].

(f) Any claim for damages caused by the imposition or establishment of a quarantine by the United States.

(g) Repealed.

(h) Any claim arising out of assault, battery, false imprisonment, false arrest, malicious prosecution, abuse of process, libel, slander, misrepresentation, deceit, or interference with contract rights: *Provided*, That, with regard to acts or omissions of investigative or law enforcement officers of the United States Government, the provisions of this chapter and section 1346(b) of this title shall apply to any claim arising, on or after the date of the enactment of this proviso, out of assault, battery, false imprisonment, false arrest, abuse of process, or malicious prosecution. For the purposes of this subsection, "investigative or law enforcement officer" means any officer of the United

States who is empowered by law to execute searches, to seize evidence, or to make arrests for violations of Federal law."

(i) Any claim for damages caused by the fiscal operations of the Treasury or by the regulation of the monetary system.

(j) Any claim arising out of the combatant activities of the military or naval forces, or the Coast Guard, during time of war.

(k) Any claim arising in a foreign country.

(l) Any claim arising from the activities of the Tennessee Valley Authority.

(m) Any claim arising from the activities of the Panama Canal Company.

(n) Any claim arising from the activities of a Federal land bank, a Federal intermediate credit bank, or a bank for cooperatives.

APPENDIX B

Judgments, Costs, and Interest

1. 28 U.S.C. § 1961. Interest

(a) Interest shall be allowed on any money judgment in a civil case recovered in a district court. Execution therefor may be levied by the marshal, in any case where, by the law of the State in which such court is held, execution may be levied for interest on judgments recovered in the courts of the State. Such interest shall be calculated from the date of the entry of the judgment, at a rate equal to the weekly average 1-year constant maturity Treasury yield, as published by the Board of Governors of the Federal Reserve System, for the calendar week preceding the date of the judgment. The Director of the Administrative Office of the United States Courts shall distribute notice of that rate and any changes in it to all Federal judges.

(b) Interest shall be computed daily to the date of payment except as provided in section 2516(b) of this title and section 1304(b) of title 31, and shall be compounded annually.

(c)(1) This section shall not apply in any judgment of any court with respect to any internal revenue tax case. Interest shall be allowed in such cases at the underpayment rate or overpayment rate (whichever is appropriate) established under section 6621 of the Internal Revenue Code of 1986.

(2) Except as otherwise provided in paragraph (1) of this subsection, interest shall be allowed on all final judgments against the United States in the United States Court of Appeals for the Federal circuit, at the rate provided in subsection (a) and as provided in subsection (b).

(3) Interest shall be allowed, computed, and paid on judgments of the United States Court of Federal Claims only as provided in paragraph (1) of this subsection or in any other provision of law.

(4) This section shall not be construed to affect the interest on any judgment of any court not specified in this section.

2. 28 U.S.C. § 2412. Costs and fees

(a)(1) Except as otherwise specifically provided by statute, a judgment for costs, as enumerated in section 1920 of this title, but not including the fees and expenses of attorneys, may be awarded to the prevailing party in any civil action brought by or against the United States or any agency and any official of the United States acting in his or her official capacity in any court having jurisdiction of such action. A judgment for costs when taxed against the United States shall, in an amount established by statute, court rule, or order, be limited to reimbursing in whole or in part the prevailing party for the costs incurred by such party in the litigation.

(2) A judgment for costs, when awarded in favor of the United States in an action brought by the United States, may include an amount equal to the filing fee prescribed under section 1914(a) of this title. The preceding sentence shall not be construed as requiring the United States to pay any filing fee.

(b) Unless expressly prohibited by statute, a court may award reasonable fees and expenses of attorneys, in addition to the costs which may be awarded pursuant to subsection (a), to the prevailing party in any civil action brought by or against the United States or any agency or any official of the United States acting in his or her official capacity in any court having jurisdiction of such action. The United States shall be liable for such fees and expenses to the same extent that any other party would be liable under the common law or under the terms of any statute which specifically provides for such an award.

(c) (1) Any judgment against the United States or any agency and any official of the United States acting in his or her official capacity for costs pursuant to subsection (a) shall be paid as provided in sections 2414 and 2517 of this title and shall be in addition to any relief provided in the judgment.

(2) Any judgment against the United States or any agency and any official of the United States acting in his or her official capacity for fees and expenses of attorneys pursuant to subsection (b) shall be paid as provided in sections 2414 and 2517 of this title, except that if the basis for the award is a finding that the United States acted in bad faith, then the award shall be paid by any agency found to have acted in bad faith and shall be in addition to any relief provided in the judgment.

(d)(1)(A) Except as otherwise specifically provided by statute, a court shall award to a prevailing party other than the United States fees and other expenses, in addition to any costs awarded pursuant to subsection (a), incurred by that party in any civil action **(other than cases sounding in tort),** including proceedings for judicial review of agency action, brought by or against the United States in any court having jurisdiction of that action, unless the court finds that the position of the United States was substantially justified or that special circumstances make an award unjust. [Emphasis added.]

* * *

(f) If the United States appeals an award of costs or fees and other expenses made against the United States under this section and the award is affirmed in whole or in part, interest shall be paid on the amount of the award as affirmed. Such interest shall be computed at the rate determined under section 1961(a) of this title, and shall run from the date of the award through the day before the date of the mandate of affirmance.

3. 28 U.S.C. § 2414. Payment of judgments and compromise settlements

Except as provided by the Contract Disputes Act of 1978, payment of final judgments rendered by a district court or the Court of International Trade against the United States shall be made on settlements by the Secretary of the Treasury. Payment of final judgments rendered by a State or foreign court or tribunal against the United States, or against its agencies or officials upon obligations or liabilities of the United States, shall be made on settlements by the Secretary of the Treasury after certification by the Attorney General that it is in the interest of the United States to pay the same.

Whenever the Attorney General determines that no appeal shall be taken from a judgment or that no further review will be sought from a decision affirming the same, he shall so certify and the judgment shall be deemed final.

Except as otherwise provided by law, compromise settlements of claims referred to the Attorney General for defense of imminent litigation or suits against the United States, or against its agencies or officials upon obligations or liabilities of the United States, made by the Attorney General or any person authorized by him, shall be settled and paid in a manner similar to judgments in like causes and appropriations or funds available for the payment of such judgments are hereby made available for the payment of such compromise settlements.

4. 28 U.S.C. § 2516. Interest on Claims and Judgments

(a) Interest on a claim against the United States shall be allowed in a judgment of the United States Court of Federal Claims only under a contract or Act of Congress expressly providing for payment thereof.

(b) Interest on a judgment against the United States affirmed by the Supreme Court after review on petition of the United States is paid at a rate equal to the weekly average 1-year constant maturity Treasury yield, as published by the Board of Governors of the Federal Reserve System, for the calendar week preceding the date of the judgment.

5. 31 U.S.C. § 1304. Judgments, awards, and compromise settlements

(a) Necessary amounts are appropriated to pay final judgments, awards, compromise settlements, and interest and costs specified in the judgments or otherwise authorized by law when—

(1) payment is not otherwise provided for;

(2) payment is certified by the Secretary of the Treasury; and

(3) the judgment, award, or settlement is payable—

(A) under section 2414, 2517, 2672, or 2677 of title 28;

(B) under section 3723 of this title;

(C) under a decision of a board of contract appeals; or

(D) in excess of an amount payable from the appropriations of an agency for a meritorious claim under section 2733 or 2734 of title 10, section 715 of title 32, or section 203 of the National Aeronautics and Space Act of 1958 (42 U.S.C.S. 2473).

(b) (1) Interest may be paid from the appropriation made by this section—

(A) on a judgment of a district court, only when the judgment becomes final after review on appeal or petition by the United States

Government, and then only from the date of filing of the transcript of the judgment with the Secretary of the Treasury through the day before the date of the mandate of affirmance; [Emphasis added.] or

(B) on a judgment of the Court of Appeals for the Federal Circuit or the United States Court of Federal Claims under section 2516(b) of title 28, only from the date of filing of the transcript of the judgment with the Secretary of the Treasury through the day before the date of the mandate of affirmance.

(2) interest payable under this subsection in a proceeding reviewed by the Supreme Court is not allowed after the end of the term in which the judgment is affirmed.

(c)(1) A judgment or compromise settlement against the Government shall be paid under this section and sections 2414, 2517, and 2518 of title 28 when the judgment or settlement arises out of an express or implied contract made by—

(A) the Army and Air Force Exchange Service;

(B) the Navy Exchanges;

(C) the Marine Corps Exchanges;

(D) the Coast Guard Exchanges; or

(E) the Exchange Councils of the National Aeronautics and Space Administration.

(2) The Exchange making the contract shall reimburse the Government for the amount paid by the Government.

APPENDIX C

Regulations

1. 28 C.F.R. Part 14

Title 28: Judicial Administration

PART 14—ADMINISTRATIVE CLAIMS UNDER FEDERAL TORT CLAIMS ACT

Section Contents

Authority: 5 U.S.C. 301; 28 U.S.C. 509, 510, and 2672.
Source: Order No. 371-66, 31 FR 16616, Dec. 29, 1966, unless otherwise noted.

§ 14.1 Scope of regulations.

These regulations shall apply only to claims asserted under the Federal Tort Claims Act. The terms Federal agency and agency, as used in this part, include the executive departments, the military departments, independent establishments of the United States, and corporations primarily acting as instrumentalities or agencies of the United States but do not include any contractor with the United States.

[Order No. 960-81, 46 FR 52355, Oct. 27, 1981]

§ 14.2 Administrative claim; when presented.

(a) For purposes of the provisions of 28 U.S.C. 2401(b), 2672, and 2675, a claim shall be deemed to have been presented when a Federal agency receives from a claimant, his duly authorized agent or legal representative, an executed Standard Form 95 or other written notification of an incident, accompanied by a claim for money damages in a sum certain for injury to or loss of property, personal injury, or death alleged to have occurred by reason of the incident; and the title or legal capacity of the person signing, and is accompanied by evidence of his authority to present a claim on behalf of the claimant as agent, executor, administrator, parent, guardian, or other representative.

(b)(1) A claim shall be presented to the Federal agency whose activities gave rise to the claim. When a claim is presented to any other Federal agency, that agency shall transfer it forthwith to the appropriate agency, if the proper agency can be identified from the claim, and advise the claimant of the transfer. If transfer is not feasible the claim shall be returned to the claimant. The fact of transfer shall not, in itself, preclude further transfer, return of the claim to the claimant or other appropriate disposition of the claim. A claim shall be presented as required by 28 U.S.C. 2401(b) as of the date it is received by the appropriate agency.

(2) When more than one Federal agency is or may be involved in the events giving rise to the claim, an agency with which the claim is filed shall contact all other affected agencies in order to designate the single agency which will thereafter investigate and decide the merits of the claim. In the event that an agreed upon designation cannot be made by the affected agencies, the Department of Justice shall be consulted and will thereafter designate an agency to investigate and decide the merits of the claim. Once a determination has been made, the designated agency shall notify the claimant that all future correspondence concerning the claim shall be directed to that Federal agency. All involved Federal agencies may agree either to conduct their own administrative reviews and to coordinate the results or to have the investigations conducted by the designated Federal agency, but, in either event, the designated Federal agency will be responsible for the final determination of the claim.

(3) A claimant presenting a claim arising from an incident to more than one agency should identify each agency to which the claim is submitted at the time each claim is presented. Where a claim arising from an incident is presented to more than one Federal agency without any indication that more than one agency is involved, and any one of the concerned Federal agencies takes final action on that claim, the final action thus taken is conclusive on the claims presented to the other agencies in regard to the time required for filing suit set forth in 28 U.S.C. 2401(b). However, if a second involved Federal agency subsequently desires to take further action with a view towards settling the claim, the second Federal agency may treat the matter as a request for reconsideration of the final denial under 28 CFR 14.9(b), unless suit has been filed in the interim, and so advise the claimant.

(4) If, after an agency final denial, the claimant files a claim arising out of the same incident with a different Federal agency, the new submission of the claim will not toll the requirement of 28 U.S.C. 2401(b) that suit must be filed within six months of the final denial by the first agency, unless the second agency specifically and explicitly treats the second submission as a request for reconsideration under 28 CFR 14.9(b) and so advises the claimant.

(c) A claim presented in compliance with paragraph (a) of this section may be amended by the claimant at any time prior to final agency action or prior to the exercise of the claimant's option under 28 U.S.C. 2675(a). Amendments shall be submitted in writing and signed by the claimant or his duly authorized agent or legal representative. Upon the timely filing of an amendment to a pending claim, the agency shall have six months in which to make a final disposition of the claim as amended and the claimant's option under 28 U.S.C. 2675(a) shall not accrue until six months after the filing of an amendment.

[Order No. 870-79, 45 FR 2650, Jan. 14, 1980, as amended by Order No. 960-81, 46 FR 52355, Oct. 27, 1981; Order No. 1179-87, 52 FR 7411, Mar. 11, 1987]

§ 14.3 Administrative claim; who may file.

(a) A claim for injury to or loss of property may be presented by the owner of the property, his duly authorized agent, or legal representative.

(b) A claim for personal injury may be presented by the injured person, his duly authorized agent, or legal representative.

(c) A claim based on death may be presented by the executor or administrator of the decendent's estate, or by any other person legally entitled to assert such a claim in accordance with applicable State law.

(d) A claim for loss wholly compensated by an insurer with the rights of a subrogee may be presented by the insurer. A claim for loss partially compensated by an insurer with the rights of a subrogee may be presented by the parties individually as their respective interests appear, or jointly.

[Order No. 371-66, 31 FR 16616, Dec. 29, 1966, as amended by Order No. 1179-87, 52 FR 7412, Mar. 11, 1987]

§ 14.4 Administrative claims; evidence and information to be submitted.

(a) Death. In support of a claim based on death, the claimant may be required to submit the following evidence or information:

(1) An authenticated death certificate or other competent evidence showing cause of death, date of death, and age of the decedent.

(2) Decedent's employment or occupation at time of death, including his monthly or yearly salary or earnings (if any), and the duration of his last employment or occupation.

(3) Full names, addresses, birth dates, kinship, and marital status of the decedent's survivors, including identification of those survivors who were dependent for support upon the decedent at the time of his death.

(4) Degree of support afforded by the decedent to each survivor dependent upon him for support at the time of his death.

(5) Decedent's general physical and mental condition before death.

(6) Itemized bills for medical and burial expenses incurred by reason of the incident causing death, or itemized receipts of payment for such expenses.

(7) If damages for pain and suffering prior to death are claimed, a physician's detailed statement specifying the injuries suffered, duration of pain and suffering, any drugs administered for pain, and the decedent's physical condition in the interval between injury and death.

(8) Any other evidence or information which may have a bearing on either the responsibility of the United States for the death or the damages claimed.

(b) Personal injury. In support of a claim for personal injury, including pain and suffering, the claimant may be required to submit the following evidence or information:

(1) A written report by his attending physician or dentist setting forth the nature and extent of the injury, nature and extent of treatment, any degree of temporary or permanent disability, the prognosis, period of hospitalization, and any diminished earning capacity. In addition, the claimant may be required to submit to a physical or mental examination by a physician employed by the agency or another Federal agency. A copy of the report of the examining physician shall be made available to the claimant upon the claimant's written request provided that he has, upon request, furnished the report referred to in the first sentence of this paragraph and has made or agrees to make available to the agency any other physician's reports previously or thereafter made of the physical or mental condition which is the subject matter of his claim.

(2) Itemized bills for medical, dental, and hospital expenses incurred, or itemized receipts of payment for such expenses.

(3) If the prognosis reveals the necessity for future treatment, a statement of expected expenses for such treatment.

(4) If a claim is made for loss of time from employment, a written statement from his employer showing actual time lost from employment, whether he is a full or part-time employee, and wages or salary actually lost.

(5) If a claim is made for loss of income and the claimant is self-employed, documentary evidence showing the amounts of earnings actually lost.

(6) Any other evidence or information which may have a bearing on either the responsibility of the United States for the personal injury or the damages claimed.

(c) Property damage. In support of a claim for injury to or loss of property, real or personal, the claimant may be required to submit the following evidence or information:

(1) Proof of ownership.

(2) A detailed statement of the amount claimed with respect to each item of property.

(3) An itemized receipt of payment for necessary repairs or itemized written estimates of the cost of such repairs.

(4) A statement listing date of purchase, purchase price, and salvage value, where repair is not economical.

(5) Any other evidence or information which may have a bearing on either the responsibility of the United States for the injury to or loss of property or the damages claimed.

§ 14.5 Review by legal officers.

The authority to adjust, determine, compromise, and settle a claim under the provisions of section 2672 of title 28, United States Code, shall, if the amount of a proposed compromise, settlement, or award exceeds $5,000, be exercised by the head of an agency or his designee only after review by a legal officer of the agency.

[Order No. 371-66, 31 FR 16616, Dec. 29, 1966, as amended by Order No. 757-77, 42 FR 62001, Dec. 8, 1977; Order No. 960-81, 46 FR 52355, Oct. 27, 1981]

§ 14.6 Dispute resolution techniques and limitations on agency authority.

(a) Guidance regarding dispute resolution. The administrative process established pursuant to 28 U.S.C. 2672 and this part 14 is intended to serve as an efficient effective forum for rapidly resolving tort claims with low costs to all participants. This guidance is provided to agencies to improve their use of this administrative process and to maximize the benefit achieved through application of prompt, fair, and efficient techniques that achieve an informal resolution of administrative tort claims without burdening claimants or the agency. This section provides guidance to agencies only and does not create or establish any right to enforce any provision of this part on behalf of any claimant against the United States, its agencies, its officers, or any other person. This section also does not require any agency to use any dispute resolution technique or process.

(1) Whenever feasible, administrative claims should be resolved through informal discussions, negotiations, and settlements rather than through the use of any formal or structured process. At the same time, agency personnel processing administrative tort claims should be trained in dispute resolution techniques and skills that can contribute to the prompt, fair, and efficient resolution of administrative claims.

(2) An agency may resolve disputed factual questions regarding claims against the United States under the FTCA, including 28 U.S.C. 2671–2680, through the use of any alternative dispute resolution technique or process if the agency specifically agrees to employ the technique or process, and reserves to itself the discretion to accept or reject the determinations made through the use of such technique or process.

(3) Alternative dispute resolution techniques or processes should not be adopted arbitrarily but rather should be based upon a determination that

use of a particular technique is warranted in the context of a particular claim or claims, and that such use will materially contribute to the prompt, fair, and efficient resolution of the claims. If alternative dispute resolution techniques will not materially contribute to the prompt, fair, and efficient resolution of claims, the dispute resolution processes otherwise used pursuant to these regulations shall be the preferred means of seeking resolution of such claims.

(b) Alternative dispute resolution —

(1) Case-by-case. In order to use, and before using, any alternative dispute resolution technique or process to facilitate the prompt resolution of disputes that are in excess of the agency's delegated authority, an agency may use the following procedure to obtain written approval from the Attorney General, or his or her designee, to compromise a claim or series of related claims.

(i) A request for settlement authority under paragraph (b)(1) of this section shall be directed to the Director, Torts Branch, Civil Division, Department of Justice, ("Director") and shall contain information justifying the request, including:

(A) The basis for concluding that liability exists under the FTCA;

(B) A description of the proposed alternative dispute resolution technique or process and a statement regarding why this proposed form of alternative dispute resolution is suitable for the claim or claims;

(C) A statement reflecting the claimant's or claimants' consent to use of the proposed form of alternative dispute resolution, indicating the proportion of any additional cost to the United States from use of the proposed alternative dispute resolution technique or process that shall be borne by the claimant or claimants, and specifying the manner and timing of payment of that proportion to be borne by the claimant or claimants;

(D) A statement of how the requested action would facilitate use of an alternative dispute resolution technique or process;

(E) An explanation of the extent to which the decision rendered in the alternative dispute resolution proceeding would be made binding upon claimants; and,

(F) An estimate of the potential range of possible settlements resulting from use of the proposed alternative dispute resolution technique.

(ii) The Director shall forward a request for expedited settlement action under paragraph (b)(1)(i) of this section, along with the Director's recommendation as to what action should be taken, to the Department of

Justice official who has authority to authorize settlement of the claim or related claims. If that official approves the request, a written authorization shall be promptly forwarded to the requesting agency.

(2) Delegation of authority. Pursuant to, and within the limits of, 28 U.S.C. 2672, the head of an agency or his or her designee may request delegations of authority to make any award, compromise, or settlement without the prior written approval of the Attorney General or his or her designee in excess of the agency's authority. In considering whether to delegate authority pursuant to 28 U.S.C. 2672 in excess of previous authority conferred upon the agency, consideration shall be given to:

(i) The extent to which the agency has established an office whose responsibilities expressly include the administrative resolution of claims presented pursuant to the Federal Tort Claims Act;

(ii) The agency's experience with the resolution of administrative claims presented pursuant to 28 U.S.C. 2672;

(iii) The Department of Justice's experiences with regard to administrative resolution of tort claims arising out of the agency's activities.

(c) Monetary authority. An award, compromise, or settlement of a claim by an agency under 28 U.S.C. 2672, in excess of $25,000 or in excess of the authority delegated to the agency by the Attorney General pursuant to 28 U.S.C. 2672, whichever is greater, shall be effected only with the prior written approval of the Attorney General or his or her designee. For purposes of this paragraph, a principal claim and any derivative or subrogated claim shall be treated as a single claim.

(d) Limitations on settlement authority—(1) Policy. An administrative claim may be adjusted, determined, compromised, or settled by an agency under 28 U.S.C. 2672 only after consultation with the Department of Justice when, in the opinion of the agency:

(i) A new precedent or a new point of law is involved; or

(ii) A question of policy is or may be involved; or

(iii) The United States is or may be entitled to indemnity or contribution from a third party and the agency is unable to adjust the third party claim; or

(iv) The compromise of a particular claim, as a practical matter, will or may control the disposition of a related claim in which the amount to be paid may exceed $25,000 or may exceed the authority delegated to the agency by the Attorney General pursuant to 28 U.S.C. 2672, whichever is greater.

(2) Litigation arising from the same incident. An administrative claim may be adjusted, determined, compromised, or settled by an agency under 28 U.S.C. 2672 only after consultation with the Department of Justice when the agency is informed or is otherwise aware that the United States or an employee, agent, or cost-plus contractor of the United States is involved in litigation based on a claim arising out of the same incident or transaction.

(e) Procedure. When Department of Justice approval or consultation is required, or the advice of the Department of Justice is otherwise to be requested, under this section, the written referral or request of the Federal agency shall be directed to the Director at any time after presentment of a claim to the Federal agency, and shall contain:

(1) A short and concise statement of the facts and of the reasons for the referral or request;

(2) Copies of relevant portions of the agency's claim file; and

(3) A statement of the recommendations or views of the agency.

[Order No. 1591-92, 57 FR 21738, May 22, 1992]

§ 14.7 [Reserved]

§ 14.8 Investigation and examination.

A Federal agency may request any other Federal agency to investigate a claim filed under section 2672, title 28, U.S. Code, or to conduct a physical examination of a claimant and provide a report of the physical examination. Compliance with such requests may be conditioned by a Federal agency upon reimbursement by the requesting agency of the expense of investigation or examination where reimbursement is authorized, as well as where it is required, by statute or regulation.

§ 14.9 Final denial of claim.

(a) Final denial of an administrative claim shall be in writing and sent to the claimant, his attorney, or legal representative by certified or registered mail. The notification of final denial may include a statement of the reasons for the denial and shall include a statement that, if the claimant is dissatisfied with the agency action, he may file suit in an appropriate U.S. District Court not later than 6 months after the date of mailing of the notification.

(b) Prior to the commencement of suit and prior to the expiration of the 6-month period provided in 28 U.S.C. 2401(b), a claimant, his duly authorized agent, or legal representative, may file a written request with the agency for reconsideration of a final denial of a claim under paragraph (a) of this section. Upon the timely filing of a request for reconsideration the agency shall have 6 months from the date of filing in which to make a final disposition of the claim and the claimant's option under 28 U.S.C. 2675(a) shall not accrue until 6 months after the filing of a request for reconsideration. Final agency action on a request for reconsideration shall be effected in accordance with the provisions of paragraph (a) of this section.

[Order No. 371-66, 31 FR 16616, Dec. 29, 1966, as amended by Order No. 422-69, 35 FR 315, Jan. 8, 1970]

§ 14.10 Action on approved claims.

(a) Any award, compromise, or settlement in an amount of $2,500 or less made pursuant to 28 U.S.C. 2672 shall be paid by the head of the Federal agency concerned out of the appropriations available to that agency. Payment of an award, compromise, or settlement in excess of $2,500 shall be obtained by the agency by forwarding Standard Form 1145 to the Claims Division, General Accounting Office. When an award is in excess of $25,000, or in excess of the authority delegated to the agency by the Attorney General pursuant to 28 U.S.C. 2672, whichever is greater, Standard Form 1145 must be accompanied by evidence that the award, compromise, or settlement has been approved by the Attorney General or his designee. When the use of Standard Form 1145 is required, it shall be executed by the claimant, or it shall be accompanied by either a claims settlement agreement or a Standard Form 95 executed by the claimant. When a claimant is represented by an attorney, the voucher for payment shall designate both the claimant and his attorney as payees; the check shall be delivered to the attorney, whose address shall appear on the voucher.

(b) Acceptance by the claimant, his agent, or legal representative, of any award, compromise or settlement made pursuant to the provisions of section 2672 or 2677 of title 28, United States Code, shall be final and conclusive on the claimant, his agent or legal representative, and any other person on whose behalf or for whose benefit the claim has been presented, and shall constitute a complete release of any claim against the United States and against any employee of the Government whose act or omission gave rise to the claim, by reason of the same subject matter.

[Order No. 371-66, 31 FR 16616, Dec. 29, 1966, as amended by Order No. 834-79, 44 FR 33399, June 11, 1979; Order No. 1591-92, 57 FR 21740, May 22, 1992]

§ 14.11 Supplementing regulations.

Each agency is authorized to issue regulations and establish procedures consistent with the regulations in this part.

Appendix to Part 14—Delegations of Settlement Authority

Delegation of Authority to the Secretary of Veterans Affairs

Section 1. Authority to Compromise Tort Claims (a) The Secretary of Veterans Affairs shall have the authority to adjust, determine, compromise, and settle a claim involving the Department of Veterans Affairs under section 2672 of title 28, United States Code, relating to the administrative settlement of federal tort claims, if the amount of the proposed adjustment, compromise, or award does not exceed $300,000. When the Secretary believes a claim pending before him presents a novel question of law or of policy, he shall obtain the advice of the Assistant Attorney General in charge of the Civil Division.

(b) The Secretary may redelegate, in writing, the settlement authority delegated to him under this section.

Section 2. Memorandum. Whenever the Secretary of Veterans Affairs settles any administrative claim pursuant to the authority granted by section 1 for an amount in excess of $100,000 and within the amount delegated to him under section 1, a memorandum fully explaining the basis for the action taken shall be executed. A copy of this memorandum shall be sent contemporaneously to the Director, FTCA Staff, Torts Branch of the Civil Division.

Delegation of Authority to the Postmaster General

Section 1. Authority to Compromise Tort Claims.

(a) The Postmaster General shall have the authority to adjust, determine, compromise, and settle a claim involving the United States Postal Service under section 2672 of title 28, United States Code, relating to the administrative settlement of federal tort claims, if the amount of the proposed adjustment, compromise, or award does not exceed $300,000. When the Postmaster General believes a claim pending before him presents a novel question of law or of policy, he shall obtain the advice of the Assistant Attorney General in charge of the Civil Division.

(b) The Postmaster General may redelegate, in writing, the settlement authority delegated to him under this section.

Section 2. Memorandum. Whenever the Postmaster General settles any administrative claim pursuant to the authority granted by section 1 for an amount in excess of $100,000 and within the amount delegated to him under section 1, a memorandum fully explaining the basis for the action taken shall be executed. A copy of this memorandum shall be sent contemporaneously to the Director, FTCA Staff, Torts Branch of the Civil Division.

Delegation of Authority to the Secretary of Defense

Section 1. Authority to Compromise Tort Claims.

(a) The Secretary of Defense shall have the authority to adjust, determine, compromise, and settle a claim involving the Department of Defense under section 2672 of title 28, United States Code, relating to the administrative settlement of federal tort claims, if the amount of the proposed adjustment, compromise, or award does not exceed $300,000. When the Secretary believes a claim pending before him presents a novel question of law or of policy, he shall obtain the advice of the Assistant Attorney General in charge of the Civil Division.

(b) The Secretary may redelegate, in writing, the settlement authority delegated to him under this section.

Section 2. Memorandum. Whenever the Secretary of Defense settles any administrative claim pursuant to the authority granted by section 1 for an amount in excess of $100,000 and within the amount delegated to him under section 1, a memorandum fully explaining the basis for the action taken shall be executed. A copy of this memorandum shall be sent contemporaneously to the Director, FTCA Staff, Torts Branch of the Civil Division.

Delegation of Authority to the Secretary of Transportation

Section 1. Authority to compromise tort claims.

(a) The Secretary of Transportation shall have the authority to adjust, determine, compromise and settle a claim involving the United States Department of Transportation under section 2672 of title 28, United States Code, relating to the administrative settlement of federal tort claims, if the amount of the proposed adjustment, compromise, or award does not exceed $100,000. When the Secretary of Transportation believes a claim pending before him presents a novel question of law or of policy, he shall obtain the advice of the Assistant Attorney General in charge of the Civil Division.

(b) The Secretary of Transportation may redelegate in writing the settlement authority delegated to him under this section.

Section 2. Memorandum. Whenever the Secretary of Transportation settles any administrative claim pursuant to the authority granted by section 1 for an amount in excess of $50,000 and within the amount delegated to him under section 1, a memorandum fully explaining the basis for the action taken shall be executed. A copy of this memorandum shall be sent to the Director, FTCA Staff, Torts Branch of the Civil Division.

Delegation of Authority to the Secretary of Health and Human Services

Section 1. Authority to Compromise Tort Claims.

(a) The Secretary of Health and Human Services shall have the authority to adjust, determine, compromise, and settle a claim involving the Department of Health and Human Services under section 2672 of title 28, United States Code, relating to the administrative settlement of federal tort claims, if the amount of the proposed adjustment, compromise, or award does not exceed $200,000. When the Secretary of Health and Human Services believes a claim pending before him presents a novel question of law or policy, he shall obtain the advice of the Assistant Attorney General in charge of the Civil Division.

(b) The Secretary of Health and Human Services may redelegate, in writing, the settlement authority delegated to him under this section.

Section 2. Memorandum. Whenever the Secretary of Health and Human Services settles any administrative claim pursuant to the authority granted by section 1 for an amount in excess of $100,000 and within the amount delegated to him under section 1, a memorandum fully explaining the basis for the action taken shall be executed. A copy of this memorandum shall be sent to the Director, FTCA Staff, Torts Branch of the Civil Division.

Delegation of Authority to the Secretary of the Department of Homeland Security Authority to Compromise Tort Claims

(a) The Secretary of the Department of Homeland Security shall have the authority to adjust, determine, compromise, and settle a claim involving the Department of Homeland Security under Section 2672 of Title 28, United States Code, relating to the administrative settlement of federal tort claims if the amount of the proposed adjustment, compromise, or award does not exceed $50,000. When the Secretary believes a claim pending before him presents a novel question of law or of policy, he shall obtain the advice of the Assistant Attorney General in charge of the Civil Division.

(b) The Secretary may redelegate, in writing, the settlement authority delegated to him under this section.

[Order No. 1302-88, 53 FR 37753, Sept. 28, 1988, as amended by Order No. 1471-91, 56 FR 4943, Feb. 7, 1991; Order No. 1482-91, 56 FR 12846, Mar. 28, 1991; Order No. 1583-92, 57 FR 13320, Apr. 16, 1992; 58 FR 36867, July 9, 1993; 61 FR 66220, Dec. 17, 1996; 68 FR 62517, Nov. 5, 2003; 73 FR 48299, Aug. 19, 2008; 73 FR 70276, 70277, Nov. 20, 2008]

2. 28 C.F.R. § 15

Title 28: Judicial Administration

PART 15—CERTIFICATION AND DECERTIFICATION IN CONNECTION WITH CERTAIN SUITS BASED UPON ACTS OR OMISSIONS OF FEDERAL EMPLOYEES AND OTHER PERSONS

Section	Contents
§ 15.1	General provisions.
§ 15.2	Expeditious delivery of process and pleadings.
§ 15.3	Agency report.
§ 15.4	Removal and defense of suits.

Authority: 5 U.S.C. 301, 8477(e)(4); 10 U.S.C. 1054, 1089; 22 U.S.C. 2702; 28 U.S.C. 509, 510, and 2679; 38 U.S.C. 7316; 42 U.S.C. 233, 2212, 2458a, and 5055(f); and the National Swine Flu Immunization Program of 1976, 90 Stat. 1113 (1976).

Source: Order No. 2697–2003, 68 FR 74188, Dec. 23, 2003, unless otherwise noted.

§ 15.1 General provisions.

(a) This part contains the regulations of the Department of Justice governing the application for and the issuance of statutory certifications and decertifications in connection with certain suits based upon the acts or omissions of Federal employees and certain other persons as to whom the remedy provided by the Federal Tort Claims Act, 28 U.S.C. 1346(b) and 2672, is made exclusive of any other civil action or proceeding for money damages by reason of the same subject matter against such Federal employees and other persons.

(b) As used in this part:

(1) Appropriate Federal agency means the Federal agency most closely associated with the program out of which the claim or suit arose. When it cannot be ascertained which Federal agency is the most closely associated with the program out of which the claim or suit arose, the responsible Director of the Torts Branch, Civil Division, Department of Justice, shall be consulted and will thereafter designate the appropriate Federal agency.

(2) Federal employee means "employee of the United States" as that term is defined by 28 U.S.C. 2671.

(3) Covered person means any person other than a Federal employee or the estate of a Federal employee as to whom Congress has provided by statute that the remedy provided by 28 U.S.C. 1346(b) and 2672 is made exclusive of any other civil action or proceeding for money damages by reason of the same subject matter against such person.

§ 15.2 Expeditious delivery of process and pleadings.

(a) Any Federal employee against whom a civil action or proceeding is brought for money damages for loss or damage to property, or personal injury or death, on account of any act or omission in the scope of the employee's office or employment with the Federal Government, shall promptly deliver all process and pleadings served on the employee, or an attested true copy thereof, to the employee's immediate superior or to whomever is designated by the head of the employee's department or agency to receive such papers. In addition, if prior to the employee's receipt of such process or pleadings, the employee receives information regarding the commencement of such a civil action or proceeding, he shall immediately so advise his superior or the designee. If the action is brought against the employee's estate this procedure shall apply to the employee's personal representative. The superior or designee shall provide the United States Attorney for the district embracing the place where the action or proceeding is brought and the responsible Branch Director of the Torts Branch, Civil Division, Department of Justice, information concerning the commencement of such action or proceeding, and copies of all process and pleadings.

(b) Any covered person against whom a civil action or proceeding is brought for money damages for loss or damage to property, or personal injury or death, on account of any act or omission, under circumstances in which Congress has provided by statute that the remedy provided by the Federal Tort Claims Act is made the exclusive remedy, shall promptly deliver to the appropriate Federal agency all process and pleadings served on the covered person, or an attested true copy thereof. In addition, if prior to the covered person's receipt of such process or pleadings, the covered person receives information regarding the commencement of such a civil action or proceeding, he shall immediately so advise the appropriate Federal agency. The appropriate Federal agency shall provide to the United States Attorney for the district embracing the place where the action or proceeding is brought, and the responsible Branch Director of the Torts Branch, Civil Division, Department of Justice, information concerning the commencement of such action or proceeding, and copies of all process and pleadings.

§ 15.3 Agency report.

(a) The Federal employee's employing Federal agency shall submit a report to the United States Attorney for the district embracing the place where the civil action or proceeding is brought fully addressing whether the employee was acting within the scope of his office or employment with the Federal Government at the time of the incident out of which the suit arose, and a copy of the report shall be sent by the employing Federal agency to the responsible Branch Director of the Torts Branch, Civil Division, Department of Justice.

(b) The appropriate Federal agency shall submit a report to the United States Attorney for the district embracing the place where the civil action or proceeding is brought fully addressing whether the person was acting as a covered person at the time of the incident out of which the suit arose, and a copy of the report shall be sent by the appropriate Federal agency to the responsible Branch Director of the Torts Branch, Civil Division, Department of Justice.

(c) A report under this section shall be submitted at the earliest possible date, or within such time as shall be fixed upon request by the United States Attorney or the responsible Branch Director of the Torts Branch.

§ 15.4 Removal and defense of suits.

(a) The United States Attorney for the district where the civil action or proceeding is brought, or any Director of the Torts Branch, Civil Division, Department of Justice, is authorized to make the statutory certification that the Federal employee was acting within the scope of his office or employment with the Federal Government at the time of the incident out of which the suit arose.

(b) The United States Attorney for the district where the civil action or proceeding is brought, or any Director of the Torts Branch, Civil Division, Department of Justice, is authorized to make the statutory certification that the covered person was acting at the time of the incident out of which the suit arose under circumstances in which Congress has provided by statute that the remedy provided by the Federal Tort Claims Act is made the exclusive remedy.

(c) A certification under this section may be withdrawn if a further evaluation of the relevant facts or the consideration of new or additional evidence calls for such action. The making, withholding, or withdrawing of certifications, and the removal and defense of, or refusal to remove or defend, such civil actions or proceedings shall be subject to the instructions and supervision of the Assistant Attorney General in charge of the Civil Division or his or her designee.

3. 28 C.F.R. Part 0, Subpart Y

[Code of Federal Regulations]
[Title 28, Volume 1]
[Revised as of July 1, 2010]
From the U.S. Government Printing Office via GPO Access
[CITE: 28CFR0]

TITLE 28—JUDICIAL ADMINISTRATION

CHAPTER I—DEPARTMENT OF JUSTICE

PART 0-ORGANIZATION OF THE DEPARTMENT OF JUSTICE—Table of Contents

Subpart Y-Authority to Compromise and Close Civil Claims and

Responsibility for Judgments, Fines, Penalties, and Forfeitures

Sec. 0.160 Offers that may be accepted by Assistant Attorneys General.

(a) Subject to the limitations set forth in paragraph (d) of this section, Assistant Attorneys General are authorized, with respect to matters assigned to their respective divisions, to:

(1) Accept offers in compromise of claims asserted by the United States in all cases in which the difference between the gross amount of the original claim and the proposed settlement does not exceed $2,000,000 or 15 percent of the original claim, whichever is greater;

(2) Accept offers in compromise of, or settle administratively, claims against the United States in all cases in which the principal amount of the proposed settlement does not exceed $2,000,000; and

(3) Accept offers in compromise in all nonmonetary cases.

(b) Subject to the limitations set forth in paragraph (d) of this section, the Assistant Attorney General, Tax Division, is further authorized to accept offers in compromise of, or settle administratively, claims against the United States, regardless of the amount of the proposed settlement, in all cases in which the Joint Committee on Taxation has indicated that it has no adverse criticism of the proposed settlement.[1]

(c) Subject to the limitations set forth in paragraph (d) of this section, the Assistant Attorney General, Environment and Natural Resources Division, is further authorized to approve settlements under the Comprehensive Environmental Response, Compensation and Liability Act, 42 U.S.C. 9601 et seq., regardless of the amount of the proposed settlement, with:

(1) Parties whose contribution to contamination at a hazardous waste site is de minimis within the meaning of 42 U.S.C. 9622(g); or

(2) Parties whose responsibility can be equitably allocated and are:

(A) Paying at least the allocated amount; or

(B) Unable to pay the allocated amount as confirmed by a qualified financial expert.

(d) Any proposed settlement, regardless of amount or circumstances, must be referred to the Deputy Attorney General or the Associate Attorney General, as appropriate:

(1) When, for any reason, the compromise of a particular claim would, as a practical matter, control or adversely influence the disposition of other claims and the compromise of all the claims taken together would exceed the authority delegated by paragraph (a) of this section; or

(2) When the Assistant Attorney General concerned is of the opinion that because of a question of law or policy presented, or because of opposition to the proposed settlement by a department or agency involved, or for any other reason, the proposed settlement should receive the personal attention of the Deputy Attorney General or the Associate Attorney General, as appropriate;

(3) When the proposed settlement converts into a mandatory duty the otherwise discretionary authority of a department or agency to promulgate, revise, or rescind regulations;

(4) When the proposed settlement commits a department or agency to expend funds that Congress has not appropriated and that have not been budgeted for the action in question, or commits a department or agency to seek particular appropriation or budget authorization; or

---

1. The smaller font is used for those portions of the regulation that are not applicable to the FTCA.

(5) When the proposed settlement otherwise limits the discretion of a department or agency to make policy or managerial decisions committed to the department or agency by Congress or by the Constitution.

[Order No. 1958-95, 60 FR 15674, Mar. 27, 1995, as amended by Order No. 3001-2008, 73 FR 54947, Sept. 24, 2008]

Sec. 0.161 Acceptance of certain offers by the Deputy Attorney General or Associate Attorney General, as appropriate.

(a) In all cases in which the acceptance of a proposed offer in compromise would exceed the authority delegated by Sec. 0.160, the Assistant Attorney General concerned shall, when he is of the opinion that the proposed offer should be accepted, transmit his recommendation to that effect to the Deputy Attorney General or the Associate Attorney General, as appropriate.

(b) The Deputy Attorney General or the Associate Attorney General, as appropriate, is authorized to exercise the settlement authority of the Attorney General as to all claims asserted by or against the United States.

[Order No. 1958-95, 60 FR 15675, Mar. 27, 1995]

Sec. 0.162 Offers which may be rejected by Assistant Attorneys General.

Each Assistant Attorney General is authorized, with respect to matters assigned to his division or office, to reject offers in compromise of any claims in behalf of the United States, or, in compromises or administrative actions to settle, against the United States, except in those cases which come under Sec. 0.160(c)(2).

[Order No. 423-69, 34 FR 20388, Dec. 31, 1969, as amended by Order No. 445-70, 35 FR 19397, Dec. 23, 1970; Order No. 960-81, 46 FR 52352, Oct. 27, 1981]

Sec. 0.163 Approval by Solicitor General of action on compromise offers in certain cases.

In any Supreme Court case the acceptance, recommendation of acceptance, or rejection, under Sec. 0.160, Sec. 0.161, or Sec. 0.162, of a compromise offer by the Assistant Attorney General concerned, shall have the approval of the Solicitor General. In any case in which the Solicitor General has authorized an appeal to any other court, a compromise offer, or any other action, which would terminate the appeal, shall be accepted or acted upon by the Assistant Attorney General concerned only upon advice from the Solicitor General that the principles of law involved do not require appellate review in that case.

Sec. 0.164 Civil claims that may be closed by Assistant Attorneys General.

Assistant Attorneys General are authorized, with respect to matters assigned to their respective divisions, to close (other than by compromise or by entry of judgment) claims asserted by the United States in all cases in which they would have authority to accept offers in compromise of such claims under Sec. 0.160(a), except:

(a) When for any reason, the closing of a particular claim would, as a practical matter, control or adversely influence the disposition of other claims and the closing of all the claims taken together would exceed the authority delegated by this section; or

(b) When the Assistant Attorney General concerned is of the opinion that because of a question of law or policy presented, or because of opposition to the proposed closing by the department or agency involved, or for any other reason, the proposed closing should receive the personal attention of the Attorney General, the Deputy Attorney General or the Associate Attorney General, as appropriate.

[Order No. 1958-95, 60 FR 15675, Mar. 27, 1995]

Sec. 0.165 Recommendations to the Deputy Attorney General or Associate Attorney General, as appropriate, that certain claims be closed.

In all cases in which the closing of a claim asserted by the United States would exceed the authority delegated by Sec. Sec. 0.160(a) and 0.164, the Assistant Attorney General concerned shall, when he is of the opinion that the claim should be closed, transmit his recommendation to that effect, together with a report on the matter, to the Deputy Attorney General or the Associate Attorney General, as appropriate, for review and final action. Such report shall be in such form as the Deputy Attorney General or the Associate Attorney General may require.

[Order No. 1958-95, 60 FR 15675, Mar. 27, 1995]

Sec. 0.166 Memorandum pertaining to closed claim.

In each case in which a claim is closed under Sec. 0.164 the Assistant Attorney General concerned shall execute and place in the file pertaining to the claim a memorandum which shall contain a description of the claim and a full statement of the reasons for closing it.

Sec. 0.167 Submission to Associate Attorney General by Director of Office of Alien Property of certain proposed allowances and disallowances.

In addition to the matters which he is required to submit to the Associate Attorney General under preceding sections of this subpart Y, the Director of the Office of Alien Property shall submit to the Associate Attorney General for such review as he may desire to make the following:

(a) Any proposed allowance by the Director, without hearing, of a title or debt claim.

(b) Any final determination of a title of debt claim, whether by allowance or disallowance.

(c) Any proposed allowance or disallowance by the Director, without hearing, of a title claim under section 9(a) of the Trading with the Enemy Act, as amended, filed less than 2 years after the date of vesting in or transfer to the Alien Property Custodian or the Attorney General of the property or interest in respect of which the claim is made:

Provided, That any such title or debt claim is within one of the following-described categories.

(1) Any title claim which involves the return of assets having a value of $50,000 or more, or any debt claim in the amount of $50,000 or more.

(2) Any title claim which will, as a practical matter, control the disposition of related title claims involving, with the principal claim, assets having a value of $50,000 or more; or any debt claim which will, as a practical matter, control the disposition of related debt claims in the aggregate amount, including the principal claim, of $50,000 or more.

(3) Any title claim or debt claim presenting a novel question of law or a question of policy which, in the opinion of the Director, should receive the personal attention of the Associate Attorney General or the Attorney General.

(d) Any sale or other disposition of vested property involving assets of $50,000 or more.

[Order No. 423-69, 34 FR 20388, Dec. 31, 1969, as amended by Order No. 445-70, 35 FR 19397, Dec. 23, 1970; Order No. 543-73, 38 FR 29587, Oct. 26, 1973; Order No. 568-74, 39 FR 18646, May 29, 1974; Order No. 699-77, 42 FR 15315, Mar. 21, 1977; Order No. 960-81, 46 FR 52352, Oct. 27, 1981]

Sec. 0.168 Redelegation by Assistant Attorneys General.

(a) Assistant Attorneys General are authorized, with respect to matters assigned to their respective divisions, to redelegate to subordinate division officials and United States Attorneys any of the authority delegated by Sec. Sec. 0.160 (a) and (b), 0.162, 0.164, and 0.172(b), except that any disagreement between a United States Attorney or other Department attorney and a client agency over a proposed settlement that cannot be resolved below the Assistant Attorney General level must be presented to the Assistant Attorney General for resolution.

(b) Redelegations of authority under this section shall be in writing and shall be approved by the Deputy Attorney General or the Associate Attorney General, as appropriate, before taking effect.

(c) Existing delegations and redelegations of authority to subordinate division officials and United States Attorneys to compromise or close civil claims shall continue in effect until modified or revoked by the respective Assistant Attorneys General.

(d) Subject to the limitations set forth in Sec. 0.160(c) and paragraph (a) of this section, redelegations by the Assistant Attorneys General to United States Attorneys may include the authority to:

(1) Accept offers in compromise of claims asserted by the United States in all cases in which the gross amount of the original claim does not exceed $5,000,000 and in which the difference between the original claim and the proposed settlement does not exceed $1,000,000; and

(2) Accept offers in compromise of, or settle administratively, claims against the United States in all cases in which the principal amount of the proposed settlement does not exceed $1,000,000.

[Order No. 1958-95, 60 FR 15675, Mar. 27, 1995]

Sec. 0.169 Definition of "gross amount of the original claim."

(a) The phrase gross amount of the original claim as used in this subpart Y and as applied to any civil fraud claim described in Sec. 0.45(d), shall mean the amount of single damages involved.

(b) The phrase gross amount of the original claim as used in this subpart Y and as applied to any civil claim brought under section 592 of the Tariff Act of 1930, as amended (see Sec. 0.45(c)), shall mean the actual amount of lost customs duties involved. In nonrevenue loss cases brought under section 592 of the Tariff Act of 1930, as amended, the phrase gross amount of the original claim shall mean the amount demanded in the Customs Service's mitigation decision issued pursuant to 19 U.S.C. 1618 or, if no mitigation decision has been issued, the gross amount of the original claim shall mean twenty percent of the dutiable value of the merchandise.

[Order No. 2343-2000, 65 FR 78414, Dec. 15, 2000]

Sec. 0.170 Interest on monetary limits.

In computing the gross amount of the original claim and the amount of the proposed settlement pursuant to this subpart Y, accrued interest shall be excluded.

Sec. 0.171 Judgments, fines, penalties, and forfeitures.

(a) Each United States Attorney shall be responsible for conducting, handling, or supervising such litigation or other actions as may be appropriate to accomplish the satisfaction, collection, or recovery of judgments, fines, penalties, and forfeitures (including bail bond forfeitures) imposed in his district, unless the Assistant Attorney General, or his delegate, of the litigating division which has jurisdiction of the case in which such judgment, fine, penalty, or forfeiture is imposed notifies the United States Attorney in writing that the division will assume such enforcement responsibilities.

(b) Each U.S. Attorney shall designate an Assistant U.S. Attorney, and such other employees as may be necessary, or shall establish an appropriate unit within his office, to be responsible for activities related to the satisfaction, collection, or recovery, as the case may be, of judgments, fines, penalties, and forfeitures (including bail-bond forfeitures).

(c) The Director of the Executive Office for United States Attorneys shall be responsible for the establishment of policy and procedures and other appropriate action to accomplish the satisfaction, collection, or recovery of fines, special assessments, penalties, interest, bail bond forfeitures, restitution, and court costs arising from the prosecution of criminal cases by the Department of Justice and the United States Attorneys. He shall also prepare regulations required by 18 U.S.C. 3613(c), pertaining to the application of tax lien provisions to criminal fines, for issuance by the Attorney General.

(d) The United States Attorney for the judicial district in which a criminal monetary penalty has been imposed is authorized to receive all notifications of payment, certified copies of judgments or orders, and notifications of change of address pertaining to an unpaid fine, which are otherwise required to be delivered to the Attorney General pursuant to 18 U.S.C. 3612. If an Assistant Attorney General of a litigating division has notified the United States Attorney, pursuant to paragraph (a) of this section that such division will assume responsibility for enforcement of a criminal monetary penalty, the United States Attorney shall promptly transmit such notifications and certified copies of judgments or orders to such division.

(e) With respect to cases assigned to his office, each United States Attorney—

(1) Shall be responsible for collection of any unpaid fine with respect to which a certification has been issued as provided in 18 U.S.C. 3612(b);

(2) Shall provide notification of delinquency or default of any fine as provided in 18 U.S.C. 3612 (d) and (e);

(3) May waive all or any part of any interest or penalty relating to a fine imposed under any prior law if, as determined by such United States Attorney, reasonable efforts to collect the interest or penalty are not likely to be effective; and

(4) Is authorized to accept delivery of the amount or property due as restitution for transfer to the victim or person eligible under 18 U.S.C. 3663 (or under 18 U.S.C. 3579 (f)(4) with respect to offenses committed prior to November 1, 1987).

(f) With respect to offenses committed after December 31, 1984, and prior to November 1, 1987, each United States Attorney is authorized with respect to cases assigned to his office—

(1) At his discretion, to declare the entire unpaid balance of a fine or penalty payable immediately in accordance with 18 U.S.C. 3565(b)(3);

(2) If a fine or penalty exceeds $500, to receive a certified copy of the judgment, otherwise required to be delivered by the clerk of the court to the Attorney General;

(3) When a fine or penalty is satisfied as provided by law,

(i) To file with the court a notice of satisfaction of judgment if the defendant makes a written request to the United States Attorney for such filing; or,

(ii) If the amount of the fine or penalty exceeds $500 to enter into a written agreement with the defendant to extend the twenty-year period of obligation to pay fine.

(g) With respect to offenses committed prior to November 1, 1987, each United States Attorney is hereby authorized, with respect to the discharge of indigent prisoners under 18 U.S.C. 3569, to make a finding as to whether the retention by a convict of property, in excess of that which is by law exempt from being taken on civil process for debt, is reasonably necessary for the convict's support or that of his family.

(h) The Director of the Bureau of Prisons shall take such steps as may be necessary to assure that the appropriate U.S. Attorney is notified whenever a prisoner is released prior to the payment of his fine.

(i) The Pardon Attorney shall notify the appropriate U.S. Attorney whenever the President issues a pardon and whenever the President remits or commutes a fine.

[Order No. 423-69, 34 FR 20388, Dec. 31, 1969, as amended by Order No. 445-70, 35 FR 19397, Dec. 23, 1970; Order No. 699-77, 42 FR 15315, Mar. 21, 1977; Order No. 960-81, 46 FR 52352, Oct. 27, 1981; Order No. 1034-83, 48 FR 50714, Nov. 3, 1983; Order No. 1413-90, 55 FR 19064, May 8, 1990]

Sec. 0.172 Authority: Federal tort claims.

(a) The Director of the Bureau of Prisons, the Commissioner of Federal Prison Industries, the Commissioner of the Immigration and Naturalization Service, the Director of the United States Marshals Service, and the Administrator of the Drug Enforcement Administration shall have authority to adjust, determine, compromise, and settle a claim involving the Bureau of Prisons, Federal Prison Industries, the Immigration and Naturalization Service, the United States Marshals Service, and the Drug Enforcement Administration, respectively, under section 2672 of title 28, United States Code, relating to the administrative settlement of Federal tort claims, if the amount of a proposed adjustment, compromise, settlement, or award does not exceed $50,000. When, in the opinion of one of those officials, such a claim pending before him presents a novel question of law or a question of policy, he shall obtain the advice of the Assistant Attorney General in charge of the Civil Division before taking action on the claim.

(b) Subject to the provisions of Sec. 0.160, the assistant Attorney General in charge of the Civil Division shall have authority to adjust, determine, compromise, and settle any other claim involving the Department under section 2672, of title 28, U.S. Code, relating to the administrative settlement of Federal tort claims.

[Order No. 423-69, 34 FR 20388, Dec. 31, 1969, as amended by Order No. 520-73, 38 FR 18381, July 10, 1973; Order No. 565-74, 39 FR 15877, May 6, 1974; Order No. 1149-86, 51 FR 31940, Sept. 8, 1986; Order No. 1528-91, 56 FR 48734, Sept. 26, 1991; Order No. 2328-2000, 65 FR 60100, Oct. 10, 2000]

Appendix to Subpart Y of Part 0—Redelegations of Authority to Compromise and Close Civil Claims

Civil Division
Redelegation of Authority, to Branch Directors, Heads of Offices, and United States Attorneys in Civil Division Cases
[Directive No. 1-10]

By virtue of the authority vested in me by part 0 of title 28 of the Code of Federal Regulations, particularly Sec. Sec. 0.45, 0.160, 0.164, and 0.168, it is hereby ordered as follows:

Section 1. Authority to Compromise or Close Cases and to File Suits and Claims

(a) Delegation to Deputy Assistant Attorneys General. The Deputy Assistant Attorneys General are authorized to act for, and to exercise the authority of, the Assistant Attorney General in charge of the Civil Division with respect to the institution of suits, the acceptance or rejection of compromise offers, and the closing of claims or cases, unless any such authority is required by law to be exercised by the Assistant Attorney General personally or has been specifically delegated to another Department official.

(b) Delegation to United States Attorneys, Branch, Office, and Staff Directors, and Attorneys-in-Charge of Field Offices. Subject to the limitations imposed by 28 CFR 0.160(c), and 0.164(a) and section 4(c) of this directive, and the authority of the Solicitor General set forth in 28 CFR 0.163,

(1) Branch, Office, and Staff Directors, and Attorneys-in-Charge of Field Offices with respect to matters assigned or delegated to their respective components are hereby delegated the authority to:

(i) Accept offers in compromise of claims on behalf of the United States in all cases in which the gross amount of the original claim does not exceed $5,000,000, so long as the difference between the gross amount of the original claim and the proposed settlement does not exceed $1,000,000;

(ii) Accept offers in compromise of, or settle administratively, claims against the United States in all cases where the principal amount of the proposed settlement does not exceed $1,000,000; and,

(iii) Reject any offers.

(2) United States Attorneys with respect to matters assigned or delegated to their respective components are hereby delegated the authority to:

(i) Accept offers in compromise of claims on behalf of the United States;

(A) In all cases in which the gross amount of the original claim does not exceed $1,000,000 and,

(B) In all cases in which the gross amount of the original claim does not exceed $5,000,000, so long as the difference between the gross amount of the original claim and the proposed settlement does not exceed $1,000,000;

(ii) Accept offers in compromise of, or settle administratively, claims against the United States in all cases where the principal amount of the proposed settlement does not exceed $1,000,000 and,

(iii) Reject any offers.

(3) With respect to claims asserted in bankruptcy proceedings, the term gross amount of the original claim in subparagraphs (1)(i) and (2)(i) of this paragraph means liquidation value. Liquidation value is the forced sale value of the collateral, if any, securing the claim(s) plus the dividend likely to be paid for the unsecured portion of the claim(s) in an actual or hypothetical liquidation of the bankruptcy estate.

(c) Subject to the limitations imposed by sections 1(e) and 4(c) of this directive, United States Attorneys, Directors, and Attorneys-in-Charge are authorized to file suits, counterclaims, and cross-claims, to close, or to take any other action necessary to protect the interests of the United States in all routine nonmonetary cases, in all routine loan collection and foreclosure cases, and in other monetary claims or cases where the gross amount of the original claim does not exceed $1,000,000. Such actions in nonmonetary cases which are other than routine will be submitted for the approval of the Assistant Attorney General, Civil Division.

(d) United States Attorneys may redelegate in writing the above-conferred compromise and suit authority to Assistant United States Attorneys who supervise other Assistant United States Attorneys who handle civil litigation.

(e) Limitations on delegations. The authority to compromise cases, file suits, counter-claims, and cross-claims, to close cases, or take any other action necessary to protect the interests of the United States, delegated by paragraphs (a) and (b) of this section, may not be exercised, and the matter shall be submitted for resolution to the Assistant Attorney General, Civil Division, when:

(1) For any reason, the proposed action, as a practical matter, will control or adversely influence the disposition of other claims totaling more than the respective amounts designated in the above paragraphs.

(2) Because a novel question of law or a question of policy is presented, or for any other reason, the proposed action should, in the opinion of the officer or employee concerned, receive the personal attention of the Assistant Attorney General, Civil Division.

(3) The agency or agencies involved are opposed to the proposed action. The views of an agency must be solicited with respect to any significant proposed action if it is a party, if it has asked to be consulted with respect to any such proposed action, or if such proposed action in a case would adversely affect any of its policies.

(4) The U.S. Attorney involved is opposed to the proposed action and requests that the matter be submitted to the Assistant Attorney General for decision.

(5) The case is on appeal, except as determined by the Director of the Appellate Staff.

Section 2. Action Memoranda

(a) Whenever, pursuant to the authority delegated by this Directive, an official of the Civil Division or a United States Attorney accepts a compromise, closes a claim, or files a suit or claim, a memorandum fully explaining the basis for the action taken shall be executed and placed in the file. In the case of matters compromised, closed, or filed by United States Attorneys, a copy of the memorandum must, upon request therefrom, be sent to the appropriate Branch or Office of the Civil Division.

(b) The compromising of cases or closing of claims or the filing of suits for claims, which a United States Attorney is not authorized to approve, shall be referred to the appropriate Branch or Office within the Civil Division, for decision by the Assistant Attorney General or the appropriate authorized person within the Civil Division. The referral memorandum should contain a detailed description of the matter, the United States Attorney's recommendation, the agency's recommendation where applicable, and a full statement of the reasons therefor.

Section 3. Return of Civil Judgment Cases to Agencies

Claims arising out of judgments in favor of the United States which cannot be permanently closed as uncollectible may be returned to the referring Federal agency for servicing and surveillance whenever all conditions set forth in USAM 4-2.230 have been met.

Section 4. Authority for Direct Reference and Delegation of Civil Division Cases to United States Attorneys

(a) Direct reference to United States Attorneys by agencies. The following civil actions under the jurisdiction of the Assistant Attorney General, Civil Division, may be referred by the agency concerned directly to the appropriate United States Attorney for handling in trial courts, subject to the limitations imposed by paragraph (c) of this section. United States Attorneys are hereby delegated the authority to take all necessary steps to protect the interests of the United States, without prior approval of the Assistant Attorney General, Civil Division, or his representatives, subject to the limitations set forth in section 1(e) of this directive. Agencies may, however, if special handling is desired, refer these cases to the Civil Division. Also, when constitutional questions or other significant issues arise in the course of such litigation, or when an appeal is taken by any party, the Civil Division should be consulted.

(1) Money claims by the United States, except claims involving penalties and forfeitures, where the gross amount of the original claim does not exceed $1,000,000.

(2) Single family dwelling house foreclosures arising out of loans made or insured by the Department of Housing and Urban Development, the Department of Veterans Affairs, and the Farm Service Agency.

(3) Suits to enjoin violations of, and to collect penalties under, the Agricultural Adjustment Act of 1938, 7 U.S.C. 1376, the Packers and Stockyards Act, 7 U.S.C. 203, 207(g), 213, 215, 216, 222, and 228a, the Perishable Agricultural Commodities Act, 1930, 7 U.S.C. 499c(a) and 499h(d), the Egg Products Inspection Act, 21 U.S.C. 1031 et seq., the Potato Research and Promotion Act, 7 U.S.C. 2611 et seq., the Cotton Research and Promotion Act of 1966, 7 U.S.C. 2101 et seq., the Federal Meat Inspection Act, 21 U.S.C. 601 et seq., and the Agricultural Marketing Agreement Act of 1937, as amended, 7 U.S.C. 601 et seq.

(4) Suits by social security beneficiaries under the Social Security Act, 42 U.S.C. 402 et seq.

(5) Social Security disability suits under 42 U.S.C. 423 et seq.

(6) Black lung beneficiary suits under the Federal Coal Mine Health and Safety Act of 1969, 30 U.S.C. 921 et seq.

(7) Suits by Medicare beneficiaries under 42 U.S.C. 1395ff.

(8) Garnishment actions authorized by 42 U.S.C. 659 for child support or alimony payments and actions for general debt, 5 U.S.C. 5520a.

(9) Judicial review of actions of the Secretary of Agriculture under the food stamp program, pursuant to the provisions of 7 U.S.C. 2022 involving retail food stores.

(10) Cases referred by the Department of Labor for the collection of penalties or for injunctive action under the Fair Labor Standards Act of 1938 and the Occupational Safety and Health Act of 1970.

(11) Cases referred by the Department of Labor solely for the collection of civil penalties under the Farm Labor Contractor Registration Act of 1963, 7 U.S.C. 2048(b).

(12) Cases referred by the Surface Transportation Board to enforce orders of the Surface Transportation Board or to enjoin or suspend such orders pursuant to 28 U.S.C. 1336.

(13) Cases referred by the United States Postal Service for injunctive relief under the nonmailable matter laws, 39 U.S.C. 3001 et seq.

(b) Delegation to United States Attorneys. Upon the recommendation of the appropriate Director, the Assistant Attorney General, Civil Division may delegate to United States Attorneys suit authority involving any claims or suits where the gross amount of the original claim does not exceed $5,000,000 where the circumstances warrant such delegations. United States Attorneys may compromise any case redelegated under this subsection in which the gross amount of the original claim does not exceed $5,000,000, so long as the difference between the gross amount of the original claim and the proposed settlement does not exceed $1,000,000. United States Attorneys may close cases redelegated to them under this subsection only upon the authorization of the appropriate authorized person within the Department of Justice. All delegations pursuant to this subsection shall be in writing and no United States Attorney shall have authority to compromise or close any such delegated case or claim except as is specified in the required written delegation or in section 1(c) of this directive. The limitations of section 1(e) of this directive also remain applicable in any case or claim delegated hereunder.

(c) Cases not covered. Regardless of the amount in controversy, the following matters normally will not be delegated to United States Attorneys for handling but will be personally or jointly handled or monitored by the appropriate Branch or Office within the Civil Division:

(1) Cases in the Court of Federal Claims.

(2) Cases within the jurisdiction of the Commercial Litigation Branch involving patents, trademarks, copyrights, etc.

(3) Cases before the United States Court of International Trade.

(4) Any case involving bribery, conflict of interest, breach of fiduciary duty, breach of employment contract, or exploitation of public office.

(5) Any fraud or False Claims Act case where the amount of single damages exceeds $1,000,000.

(6) Any case involving vessel-caused pollution in navigable waters.

(7) Cases on appeal, except as determined by the Director of the Appellate Staff.

(8) Any case involving litigation in a foreign court.

(9) Criminal proceedings arising under statutes enforced by the Food and Drug Administration, the Consumer Product Safety Commission, the Federal Trade Commission, and the National Highway Traffic Safety Administration (relating to odometer tampering), except as determined by the Director of the Office of Consumer Litigation.

(10) Nonmonetary civil cases, including injunction suits, declaratory judgment actions, and applications for inspection warrants, and cases seeking civil penalties including but not limited to those arising under statutes enforced by the Food and Drug Administration, the Consumer Product

Safety Commission, the Federal Trade Commission, and the National High-way Traffic Safety Administration (relating to odometer tampering), except as determined by the Director of the Office of Consumer Litigation.

(11) Administrative claims arising under the Federal Tort Claims Act.

Section 5. Civil Investigative Demands

Authority relating to Civil Investigative Demands issued under the False Claims Act is hereby delegated to United States Attorneys in cases that are delegated or assigned as monitored to their respective components. In accordance with guidelines provided by the Assistant Attorney General, each United States Attorney must provide notice and a report of Civil Investigative Demands issued by the United States Attorney. When a case is jointly handled by the Civil Division and a United States Attorney's Office, the Civil Division will issue a Civil Investigative Demand only after requesting the United States Attorney's recommendation.

Section 6. Adverse Decisions

All final judicial decisions adverse to the Government involving any direct reference or delegated case must be reported promptly to the Assistant Attorney General, Civil Division, attention Director, Appellate Staff. Consult title 2 of the United States Attorney's Manual for procedures and time limitations. An appeal cannot be taken without approval of the Solicitor General. Until the Solicitor General has made a decision whether an appeal will be taken, the Government attorney handling the case must take all necessary procedural actions to preserve the Government's right to take an appeal, including filing a protective notice of appeal when the time to file a notice of appeal is about to expire and the Solicitor General has not yet made a decision. Nothing in the foregoing directive affects this obligation.

Section 7. Supersession

This directive supersedes Civil Division Directive No. 14-95 regarding redelegation of the Assistant Attorney General's authority in Civil Division cases to Branch Directors, heads of offices, and United States Attorneys.

Section 8. Applicability

This directive applies to all cases pending as of the date of this directive and is effective immediately.

Section 9. No Private Right of Action

This directive consists of rules of agency organization, procedure, and practice and does not create a private right of action for any private party to challenge the rules or actions taken pursuant to them.

4. 28 C.F.R. § 50.15

[Code of Federal Regulations]
[Title 28, Volume 2]
[Revised as of July 1, 2010]
From the U.S. Government Printing Office via GPO Access
[CITE: 28 CFR 50.15]

TITLE 28—JUDICIAL ADMINISTRATION
CHAPTER I—DEPARTMENT OF JUSTICE (CONTINUED)
PART 50 STATEMENTS OF POLICY—Table of Contents

Sec. 50.15 Representation of Federal officials and employees by Department of Justice attorneys or by private counsel furnished by the Department in civil, criminal, and congressional proceedings in which Federal employees are sued, subpoenaed, or charged in their individual capacities.

(a) Under the procedures set forth below, a Federal employee (hereby defined to include present and former Federal officials and employees) may be provided representation in civil, criminal, and Congressional proceedings in which he is sued, subpoenaed, or charged in his individual capacity, not covered by Sec. 15.1 of this chapter, when the actions for which representation is requested reasonably appear to have been performed within the scope of the employee's employment and the Attorney General or his designee determines that providing representation would otherwise be in the interest of the United States. No special form of request for representation is required when it is clear from the proceedings in a case that the employee is being sued solely in his official capacity and only equitable relief is sought. (See USAM 4-13.000)

(1) When an employee believes he is entitled to representation by the Department of Justice in a proceeding, he must submit forthwith a written request for that representation, together with all process and pleadings served upon him, to his immediate supervisor or whomever is designated

by the head of his department or agency. Unless the employee's employing Federal agency concludes that representation is clearly unwarranted, it shall submit, in a timely manner, to the Civil Division or other appropriate litigating division (Antitrust, Civil Rights, Criminal, Land and Natural Resources, or the Tax Division), a statement containing its findings as to whether the employee was acting within the scope of his employment and its recommendation for or against providing representation. The statement should be accompanied by all available factual information. In emergency situations the litigating division may initiate conditional representation after a telephone request from the appropriate official of the employing agency. In such cases, the written request and appropriate documentation must be subsequently provided.

(2) Upon receipt of the individual's request for counsel, the litigating division shall determine whether the employee's actions reasonably appear to have been performed within the scope of his employment and whether providing representation would be in the interest of the United States. In circumstances where considerations of professional ethics prohibit direct review of the facts by attorneys of the litigating division (e.g., because of the possible existence of inter-defendant conflicts) the litigating division may delegate the fact-finding aspects of this function to other components of the Department or to a private attorney at federal expenses.

(3) Attorneys employed by any component of the Department of Justice who participate in any process utilized for the purpose of determining whether the Department should provide representation to a Federal employee, undertake a full and traditional attorney-client relationship with the employee with respect to application of the attorney-client privilege. If representation is authorized, Justice Department attorneys who represent an employee under this section also undertake a full and traditional attorney-client relationship with the employee with respect to the attorney-client privilege. Any adverse information communicated by the client-employee to an attorney during the course of such attorney-client relationship shall not be disclosed to anyone, either inside or outside the Department, other than attorneys responsible for representation of the employee, unless such disclosure is authorized by the employee. Such adverse information shall continue to be fully protected whether or not representation is provided, and even though representation may be denied or discontinued. The extent, if any, to which attorneys employed by an agency other than the Department of Justice undertake a full and traditional attorney-client relationship with the

employee with respect to the attorney-client privilege, either for purposes of determining whether representation should be provided or to assist Justice Department attorneys in representing the employee, shall be determined by the agency employing the attorneys.

(4) Representation generally is not available in federal criminal proceedings. Representation may be provided to a Federal employee in connection with a federal criminal proceeding only where the Attorney General or his designee determines that representation is in the interest of the United States and subject to applicable limitations of Sec. 50.16. In determining whether representation in a federal criminal proceeding is in the interest of the United States, the Attorney General or his designee shall consider, among other factors, the relevance of any non-prosecutorial interests of the United States, the importance of the interests implicated, the Department's ability to protect those interests through other means, and the likelihood of a conflict of interest between the Department's prosecutorial and representational responsibilities. If representation is authorized, the Attorney General or his designee also may determine whether representation by Department attorneys, retention of private counsel at federal expense, or reimbursement to the employee of private counsel fees is most appropriate under the circumstances.

(5) Where representation is sought for proceedings other than federal criminal proceedings, but there appears to exist the possibility of a federal criminal investigation or indictment relating to the same subject matter, the litigating division shall contact a designated official in the Criminal, Civil Rights, or Tax Division or other prosecutive authority within the Department (hereinafter "prosecuting division") to determine whether the employee is either a subject of a federal criminal investigation or a defendant in a federal criminal case. An employee is the subject of an investigation if, in addition to being circumstantially implicated by having the appropriate responsibilities at the appropriate time, there is some evidence of his specific participation in a crime.

(6) If a prosecuting division of the Department indicates that the employee is not the subject of a criminal investigation concerning the act or acts for which he seeks representation, then representation may be provided if otherwise permissible under the provisions of this section. Similarly, if the prosecuting division indicates that there is an ongoing investigation, but into a matter unrelated to that for which representation has been requested, then representation may be provided.

(7) If the prosecuting division indicates that the employee is the subject of a federal criminal investigation concerning the act or acts for which he seeks representation, the litigating division shall inform the employee that no representation by Justice Department attorneys will be provided in that federal criminal proceeding or in any related civil, congressional, or state criminal proceeding. In such a case, however, the litigating division, in its discretion, may provide a private attorney to the employee at federal expense under the procedures of Sec. 50.16, or provide reimbursement to employees for private attorney fees incurred in connection with such related civil, congressional, or state criminal proceeding, provided no decision has been made to seek an indictment or file an information against the employee.

(8) In any case where it is determined that Department of Justice attorneys will represent a Federal employee, the employee must be notified of his right to retain private counsel at his own expense. If he elects representation by Department of Justice attorneys, the employee and his agency shall be promptly informed:

(i) That in actions where the United States, any agency, or any officer thereof in his official capacity is also named as a defendant, the Department of Justice is required by law to represent the United States and/or such agency or officer and will assert all appropriate legal positions and defenses on behalf of such agency, officer, and/or the United States;

(ii) That the Department of Justice will not assert any legal position or defense on behalf of any employee sued in his individual capacity which is deemed not to be in the interest of the United States;

(iii) Where appropriate, that neither the Department of Justice nor any agency of the U.S. Government is obligated to pay or to indemnify the defendant employee for any judgment for money damages which may be rendered against such employee; but that, where authorized, the employee may apply for such indemnification from his employing agency upon the entry of an adverse verdict, judgment, or other monetary award;

(iv) That any appeal by Department of Justice attorneys from an adverse ruling or judgment against the employee may only be taken upon the discretionary approval of the Solicitor General, but the employee-defendant may pursue an appeal at his own expense whenever the Solicitor General declines to authorize an appeal and private counsel is not provided at federal expense under the procedures of Sec. 50.16; and

(v) That while no conflict appears to exist at the time representation is tendered which would preclude making all arguments necessary to the adequate defense of the employee, if such conflict should arise in the future the employee will be promptly advised and steps will be taken to resolve the conflict as indicated by paragraph (a) (6), (9) and (10) of this section, and by Sec. 50.16.

(9) If a determination not to provide representation is made, the litigating division shall inform the agency and/or the employee of the determination.

(10) If conflicts exist between the legal and factual positions of various employees in the same case which make it inappropriate for a single attorney to represent them all, the employees may be separated into as many compatible groups as is necessary to resolve the conflict problem and each group may be provided with separate representation. Circumstances may make it advisable that private representation be provided to all conflicting groups and that direct Justice Department representation be withheld so as not to prejudice particular defendants. In such situations, the procedures of Sec. 50.16 will apply.

(11) Whenever the Solicitor General declines to authorize further appellate review or the Department attorney assigned to represent an employee becomes aware that the representation of the employee could involve the assertion of a position that conflicts with the interests of the United States, the attorney shall fully advise the employee of the decision not to appeal or the nature, extent, and potential consequences of the conflict. The attorney shall also determine, after consultation with his supervisor (and, if appropriate, with the litigating division) whether the assertion of the position or appellate review is necessary to the adequate representation of the employee and

(i) If it is determined that the assertion of the position or appeal is not necessary to the adequate representation of the employee, and if the employee knowingly agrees to forego appeal or to waive the assertion of that position, governmental representation may be provided or continued; or

(ii) If the employee does not consent to forego appeal or waive the assertion of the position, or if it is determined that an appeal or assertion of the position is necessary to the adequate representation of the employee, a Justice Department lawyer may not provide or continue to provide the representation; and

(iii) In appropriate cases arising under paragraph (a)(10)(ii) of this section, a private attorney may be provided at federal expense under the procedures of Sec. 50.16.

(12) Once undertaken, representation of a Federal employee under this subsection will continue until either all appropriate proceedings, including applicable appellate procedures approved by the Solicitor General, have ended, or until any of the bases for declining or withdrawing from representation set forth in this section is found to exist, including without limitation the basis that representation is not in the interest of the United States. If representation is discontinued for any reason, the representing Department attorney on the case will seek to withdraw but will take all reasonable steps to avoid prejudice to the employee.

(b) Representation is not available to a Federal employee whenever:

(1) The conduct with regard to which the employee desires representation does not reasonably appear to have been performed within the scope of his employment with the Federal government;

(2) It is otherwise determined by the Department that it is not in the interest of the United States to provide representation to the employee.

(c)(1) The Department of Justice may indemnify the defendant Department of Justice employee for any verdict, judgment, or other monetary award which is rendered against such employee, provided that the conduct giving rise to the verdict, judgment, or award was taken within the scope of employment and that such indemnification is in the interest of the United States, as determined by the Attorney General or his designee.

(2) The Department of Justice may settle or compromise a personal damages claim against a Department of Justice employee by the payment of available funds, at any time, provided the alleged conduct giving rise to the personal damages claim was taken within the scope of employment and that such settlement or compromise is in the interest of the United States, as determined by the Attorney General or his designee.

(3) Absent exceptional circumstances as determined by the Attorney General or his designee, the Department will not entertain a request either to agree to indemnify or to settle a personal damages claim before entry of an adverse verdict, judgment, or award.

(4) The Department of Justice employee may request indemnification to satisfy a verdict, judgment, or award entered against the employee. The employee shall submit a written request, with appropriate documentation including copies of the verdict, judgment, award, or settlement proposal if on appeal, to the head of his employing component, who shall thereupon submit to the appropriate Assistant Attorney General, in a timely manner, a

recommended disposition of the request. Where appropriate, the Assistant Attorney General shall seek the views of the U.S. Attorney; in all such cases the Civil Division shall be consulted. The Assistant Attorney General shall forward the request, the employing component's recommendation, and the Assistant Attorney General's recommendation to the Attorney General for decision.

(5) Any payment under this section either to indemnify a Department of Justice employee or to settle a personal damages claim shall be contingent upon the availability of appropriated funds of the employing component of the Department of Justice.

[Order No. 970-82, 47 FR 8172, Feb. 25, 1982, as amended at Order No. 1139-86, 51 FR 27022, July 29, 1986; Order No. 1409-90, 55 FR 13130, Apr. 9, 1990]

APPENDIX D

Standard Form 95

This is the two-page Standard Form for submission of an FTCA Administrative Claim. It is available from many agencies. A fillable PDF version is available at https://www.gsa.gov/cdnstatic/SF95-07a.pdf?forceDownload=1.

CLAIM FOR DAMAGE, INJURY, OR DEATH	INSTRUCTIONS: Please read carefully the instructions on the reverse side and supply information requested on both sides of this form. Use additional sheet(s) if necessary. See reverse side for additional instructions.	FORM APPROVED OMB NO. 1105-0008

1. Submit to Appropriate Federal Agency:	2. Name, address of claimant, and claimant's personal representative if any. (See instructions on reverse). Number, Street, City, State and Zip code.

3. TYPE OF EMPLOYMENT ☐ MILITARY ☐ CIVILIAN	4. DATE OF BIRTH	5. MARITAL STATUS	6. DATE AND DAY OF ACCIDENT	7. TIME (A.M. OR P.M.)

8. BASIS OF CLAIM (State in detail the known facts and circumstances attending the damage, injury, or death, identifying persons and property involved, the place of occurrence and the cause thereof. Use additional pages if necessary).

9. **PROPERTY DAMAGE**

NAME AND ADDRESS OF OWNER, IF OTHER THAN CLAIMANT (Number, Street, City, State, and Zip Code).

BRIEFLY DESCRIBE THE PROPERTY, NATURE AND EXTENT OF THE DAMAGE AND THE LOCATION OF WHERE THE PROPERTY MAY BE INSPECTED. (See instructions on reverse side).

10. **PERSONAL INJURY/WRONGFUL DEATH**

STATE THE NATURE AND EXTENT OF EACH INJURY OR CAUSE OF DEATH, WHICH FORMS THE BASIS OF THE CLAIM. IF OTHER THAN CLAIMANT, STATE THE NAME OF THE INJURED PERSON OR DECEDENT.

11. **WITNESSES**

NAME	ADDRESS (Number, Street, City, State, and Zip Code)

12. (See instructions on reverse).	AMOUNT OF CLAIM (in dollars)		
12a. PROPERTY DAMAGE	12b. PERSONAL INJURY	12c. WRONGFUL DEATH	12d. TOTAL (Failure to specify may cause forfeiture of your rights).

I CERTIFY THAT THE AMOUNT OF CLAIM COVERS ONLY DAMAGES AND INJURIES CAUSED BY THE INCIDENT ABOVE AND AGREE TO ACCEPT SAID AMOUNT IN FULL SATISFACTION AND FINAL SETTLEMENT OF THIS CLAIM.

13a. SIGNATURE OF CLAIMANT (See instructions on reverse side).	13b. PHONE NUMBER OF PERSON SIGNING FORM	14. DATE OF SIGNATURE

CIVIL PENALTY FOR PRESENTING FRAUDULENT CLAIM	CRIMINAL PENALTY FOR PRESENTING FRAUDULENT CLAIM OR MAKING FALSE STATEMENTS
The claimant is liable to the United States Government for a civil penalty of not less than $5,000 and not more than $10,000, plus 3 times the amount of damages sustained by the Government. (See 31 U.S.C. 3729).	Fine, imprisonment, or both. (See 18 U.S.C. 287, 1001.)

Authorized for Local Reproduction Previous Edition is not Usable 95-109	NSN 7540-00-634-4046	STANDARD FORM 95 (REV. 2/2007) PRESCRIBED BY DEPT. OF JUSTICE 28 CFR 14.2

INSURANCE COVERAGE

In order that subrogation claims may be adjudicated, it is essential that the claimant provide the following information regarding the insurance coverage of the vehicle or property.

15. Do you carry accident insurance? ☐ Yes   If yes, give name and address of insurance company (Number, Street, City, State, and Zip Code) and policy number. ☐ No

16. Have you filed a claim with your insurance carrier in this instance, and if so, is it full coverage or deductible? ☐ Yes ☐ No   17. If deductible, state amount.

18. If a claim has been filed with your carrier, what action has your insurer taken or proposed to take with reference to your claim? (It is necessary that you ascertain these facts).

19. Do you carry public liability and property damage insurance? ☐ Yes   If yes, give name and address of insurance carrier (Number, Street, City, State, and Zip Code). ☐ No

INSTRUCTIONS

Claims presented under the Federal Tort Claims Act should be submitted directly to the "appropriate Federal agency" whose employee(s) was involved in the incident. If the incident involves more than one claimant, each claimant should submit a separate claim form.

Complete all items - Insert the word NONE where applicable.

A CLAIM SHALL BE DEEMED TO HAVE BEEN PRESENTED WHEN A FEDERAL AGENCY RECEIVES FROM A CLAIMANT, HIS DULY AUTHORIZED AGENT, OR LEGAL REPRESENTATIVE, AN EXECUTED STANDARD FORM 95 OR OTHER WRITTEN NOTIFICATION OF AN INCIDENT, ACCOMPANIED BY A CLAIM FOR MONEY DAMAGES IN A SUM CERTAIN FOR INJURY TO OR LOSS OF PROPERTY, PERSONAL INJURY, OR DEATH ALLEGED TO HAVE OCCURRED BY REASON OF THE INCIDENT. THE CLAIM MUST BE PRESENTED TO THE APPROPRIATE FEDERAL AGENCY WITHIN TWO YEARS AFTER THE CLAIM ACCRUES.

Failure to completely execute this form or to supply the requested material within two years from the date the claim accrued may render your claim invalid. A claim is deemed presented when it is received by the appropriate agency, not when it is mailed.

If instruction is needed in completing this form, the agency listed in item #1 on the reverse side may be contacted. Complete regulations pertaining to claims asserted under the Federal Tort Claims Act can be found in Title 28, Code of Federal Regulations, Part 14. Many agencies have published supplementing regulations. If more than one agency is involved, please state each agency.

The claim may be filled by a duly authorized agent or other legal representative, provided evidence satisfactory to the Government is submitted with the claim establishing express authority to act for the claimant. A claim presented by an agent or legal representative must be presented in the name of the claimant. If the claim is signed by the agent or legal representative, it must show the title or legal capacity of the person signing and be accompanied by evidence of his/her authority to present a claim on behalf of the claimant as agent, executor, administrator, parent, guardian or other representative.

If claimant intends to file for both personal injury and property damage, the amount for each must be shown in item number 12 of this form.

The amount claimed should be substantiated by competent evidence as follows:

(a) In support of the claim for personal injury or death, the claimant should submit a written report by the attending physician, showing the nature and extent of the injury, the nature and extent of treatment, the degree of permanent disability, if any, the prognosis, and the period of hospitalization, or incapacitation, attaching itemized bills for medical, hospital, or burial expenses actually incurred.

(b) In support of claims for damage to property, which has been or can be economically repaired, the claimant should submit at least two itemized signed statements or estimates by reliable, disinterested concerns, or, if payment has been made, the itemized signed receipts evidencing payment.

(c) In support of claims for damage to property which is not economically repairable, or if the property is lost or destroyed, the claimant should submit statements as to the original cost of the property, the date of purchase, and the value of the property, both before and after the accident. Such statements should be by disinterested competent persons, preferably reputable dealers or officials familiar with the type of property damaged, or by two or more competitive bidders, and should be certified as being just and correct.

(d) Failure to specify a sum certain will render your claim invalid and may result in forfeiture of your rights.

PRIVACY ACT NOTICE

This Notice is provided in accordance with the Privacy Act, 5 U.S.C. 552a(e)(3), and concerns the information requested in the letter to which this Notice is attached.
A. Authority: The requested information is solicited pursuant to one or more of the following: 5 U.S.C. 301, 28 U.S.C. 501 et seq., 28 U.S.C. 2671 et seq., 28 C.F.R. Part 14.

B. Principal Purpose: The information requested is to be used in evaluating claims.
C. Routine Use: See the Notices of Systems of Records for the agency to whom you are submitting this form for this information.
D. Effect of Failure to Respond: Disclosure is voluntary. However, failure to supply the requested information or to execute this form may render your claim "invalid."

PAPERWORK REDUCTION ACT NOTICE

This notice is solely for the purpose of the Paperwork Reduction Act, 44 U.S.C. 3501. Public reporting burden for this collection of information is estimated to average 6 hours per response, including the time for reviewing instructions, searching existing data sources, gathering and maintaining the data needed, and completing and reviewing the collection of information. Send comments regarding this burden estimate or any other aspect of this collection of information, including suggestions for reducing this burden, to the Director, Torts Branch, Attention: Paperwork Reduction Staff, Civil Division, U.S. Department of Justice, Washington, DC 20530 or to the Office of Management and Budget. Do not mail completed form(s) to these addresses.

STANDARD FORM 95 REV. (2/2007) BACK

APPENDIX E

Filing Transcript of Judgment

Contact information for the Judgment Fund Section in the Bureau of the Fiscal Service:

Phone: (202) 874-6664
Toll-Free Number: 1-866-277-1046
E-mail: judgment.fund@fiscal.treasury.gov

Address:
Department of the Treasury
Fiscal Service
Judgment Fund Branch
3201 Pennsy Drive
Building E
Landover, MD 20785

1. Sample Letter

Date: _____

Department of the Treasury
Fiscal Service
Judgment Fund Branch
3201 Pennsy Drive
Building E
Landover, MD 20785

    Re: (Case Name and Court Docket No.)

Dear Sir or Madam:

I am the authorized representative of the plaintiff in the captioned Federal Tort Claims Act matter. With this letter I am filing the attached transcript of judgment payable by the United States. I am submitting this transcript of judgment to preserve rights to interest under 31 U.S.C. § 1304. Counsel for the United States was provided a copy of this correspondence.

Thank you for your prompt attention to this matter.

Cordially yours,

(Name, Title, and Organization)

Enclosures

cc: Opposing counsel,

Full address of opposing counsel

APPENDIX F

Checklist of FTCA Defenses

"[T]he United States, as sovereign, 'is immune from suit, save as it consents to be sued . . . and the terms of its consent to be sued in any court define that court's jurisdiction to entertain the suit.'" *United States v. Testan*, 424 U.S. 392, 399 (1976) (quoting *United States v. Sherwood*, 312 U.S. 584, 586 (1941))

I. Prerequisites for suit under the FTCA
   A. Administrative claim
      1. No administrative claim filed. (28 U.S.C. § 2675(a)). Class action cannot be maintained unless each class member files an administrative claim.
      2. Claim is not for a Sum Certain in Damages (28 CFR § 14.2(a)). Ad Damnum in subsequent suit cannot exceed the amount claimed administratively absent newly discovered evidence. (28 U.S.C. § 2675(b)).
      3. Claim not filed in writing by claimant or duly authorized legal representative or agent. (28 CFR § 14.3).
      4. Claimant does not identify the time, place, or tortfeasor.
      5. Insufficient supporting information supplied with claim. (28 CFR § 14.4) (minority position).
      6. Suit filed before final denial received from agency or six months from date administrative claim filed. (28 U.S.C. § 2675(a)).
   B. Statute of limitations (28 U.S.C. § 2401(b)).
      1. Administrative claim not filed within two years of accrual.
      2. Suit not filed within six months of denial of administrative claim.
      3. Statutes of Repose applicable to private person defendants.

II. Procedural limits of the FTCA
   A. Suit must be filed in Federal district court. (28 U.S.C. § 1346(b)(1)).

B. Suit must be filed in Federal district where plaintiff is domiciled or where act or omission occurred. (28 U.S.C. § 1402(b)).

C. Attorney General and U.S. Attorney must be properly served. (Fed. R. Civ. P. 4(i)(1)).

D. Actions against the United States cannot be tried to a jury. (28 U.S.C. § 2402).

E. Only the United States can be sued (28 U.S.C. § 1346(b)(1)); Agencies and Federal Employees in their official capacities cannot be sued *eo nomine*. (28 U.S.C. § 2679(a)).

III. The FTCA is the exclusive remedy for suits against the United States or its agencies sounding in tort. (28 U.S.C. §§ 1346(b)(1)).

A. The United States cannot be sued in tort directly under the Constitution, under diversity jurisdiction, under 42 U.S.C. § 1983, or under a pendent jurisdiction theory.

B. Matters not encompassed by the FTCA's waiver of sovereign immunity.

1. Tortfeasor is not an employee of the United States.
(Does not fall within 28 U.S.C. § 2671 definition or the government does not control detailed physical aspects of personal service contractors' operations).

a. Employees of Contractors.

i. FTCA definition of "agency" "does not include any contractor with the United States." (28 U.S.C. § 2671).

ii. Claim is based on vicarious liability or nondelegable duty theory.

b. Employees of the District of Columbia, the government of the Virgin Islands, etc.

c. Borrowed servant doctrine.

2. Tort committed while tortfeasor acting outside the scope of employment.

3. Suit does not allege a tort under state law that is based on negligent or wrongful conduct.

a. Claim is based on strict or absolute liability. (28 U.S.C. § 1346(b)(1)).

b. Private party not liable under like circumstances under the applicable state law. (28 U.S.C. §§ 1346(b)(1), 2674).

i. No tort under state law.

ii. Affirmative defenses under state law [*e.g.*, contributory or comparative negligence; assumption of risk; recreational use statute; workers' compensation (United States as principal or statutory employer)].

iii. Claim is based on the violation of a duty imposed by Federal statute or regulation.

iv. Private parties do not engage in analogous activity—conduct challenged involves a core governmental activity.

c. Claim is actually a taking claim, or one essentially contractual in nature—jurisdiction in Court of Federal Claims. (§ 1346(a)).

4. *Feres* doctrine.

a. Claim arising incident to military service.

b. Claim of service member arising from core military decision or management of other military members.

IV. Statutory bars to sovereign immunity

A. FTCA exceptions (28 U.S.C. § 2680)

a. 1. Due care in the exercise of a statute or regulation.

2. Discretionary function exception.

b. Arises out of transmission of postal matter.

c. Arises with respect to assessment or collection of a tax or customs duty or from the detention of goods by a law enforcement officer, excise officer, or customs officer if:

1. property seized for purpose of forfeiture under provision of Federal law providing for the forfeiture of property other than as a sentence imposed upon conviction of a criminal offense;

2. the interest of the claimant was not forfeited;

3. the interest of the claimant was not remitted or mitigated (if the property was subject to forfeiture); and

4. the claimant was not convicted of a crime for which the interest of the claimant in the property was subject to forfeiture under a Federal criminal forfeiture law.

d. Cognizable under the suits in Admiralty Act or Public Vessels Act.

e. Arises from the Administration of Trading with the Enemy Act.

f. Damages from the imposition or establishment of a quarantine.

g. [REPEALED].

h. Arises out of assault and battery, false arrest or imprisonment, malicious prosecution or abuse of process committed by one other than a law enforcement officer, or arises from libel, slander, misrepresentation, or deceit; interference with contract rights.

i. Arises from fiscal operations of the Treasury Department or regulation of the monetary system.

j. Arises from the combatant activities of the Armed Forces during time of war.

k. Arises in a foreign country.

l. Arises from the activities of the Tennessee Valley Authority.

m. Arises from activities of the Panama Canal Company.

n. Arises from activities of a cooperative bank, a Federal Land Bank or a Federal Intermediate Credit Bank.

B. General statutory bars to FTCA liability

(This is a non-exhaustive list.)

1. Claim for damages from flood control operations. (33 U.S.C. § 702(c)).

2. Claim challenging Social Security decision. (42 U.S.C. § 405 (h)).

3. Claim challenging Medicare decision. (42 U.S.C. § 405(g) and (h)).

4. Claim challenging Veterans' Administration decision. (38 U.S.C. § 511).

5. Claims brought by Non-Resident Enemy Aliens in Time of War. (50 U.S.C. App. § 7(b)).

6. Claim based on navigational aid from National Geospatial-Intelligence Agency. (10 U.S.C. § 456).

7. Claim arising from Panama Canal Commission not involving ship in transit. (22 U.S.C. § 3761).

8. Claim of prisoner for emotional distress. (28 U.S.C. § 1346(b)(2)).

C. Exclusive alternative remedy bars to suit

(This is a non-exhaustive list.)

1. Federal Employees Compensation Act. (5 U.S.C. § 8116(c)).

2. Longshoremen's and Harbor Workers Compensation Act— Employees not covered by FECA. (33 U.S.C. § 905(a)).

3. Civil Service Reform Act. (Pub. L. No. 95-454).

4. Clean Water Act. (33 U.S.C. § 1365).

5. Compensation from Federal Prison Industries Fund. (18 U.S.C. § 4126).

6. Public Vessels Act. (46 U.S.C. § 31102).

7. NATO Status of Forces Agreement. (4 U.S.T. 1792).

8. Veterans Administration Benefits—exclusive remedy for injuries incurred incident to military service.

D. Assigned claims—barred by Anti-Assignment Act. (31 U.S.C. § 3727).

V. Damages

(This is a non-exhaustive list.)

A. Amount sought exceeds the amount claimed administratively. (28 U.S.C. § 2675(b)).

B. Suit seeks punitive damages or other non-compensatory relief. (28 U.S.C. § 2674).

C. Applicable state law puts cap on damages.

D. Applicable state law does not recognize claimed element of damages.

E. Applicable state law requires reduction for plaintiff's fault.

F. Award sought is not reduced to reflect future tax liability.

G. Award sought is not discounted to present value.

H. Award sought is not reduced to reflect non-collateral payments.

I. Duplicative awards—overlapping elements of damages.

J. Failure to mitigate damages.

K. Prejudgment interest sought. (28 U.S.C. § 2674).

L. Post-judgment interest sought in situations not authorized by 31 U.S.C. § 1304.

VI. Settlement or release

(This is a non-exhaustive list.)

A. Acceptance of settlement offer. (28 U.S.C. § 2672; 28 CFR § 14.10(b)).

B. Contractual release from future liability or covenant not to sue.

C. Recovery from, or release of, joint tortfeasor.

APPENDIX G

Checklist for Filing Administrative Tort Claim

1. No later than two years after your claim accrued, a written claim must arrive at the offices of the Federal agency whose action gives rise to the claim. Otherwise your claim will be "forever barred." 28 U.S.C. § 2401(b).

2. Complete Standard Form 95 (copy at Appendix D).

Fill the form out as completely as possible. Take special care with the following blocks.

In Block 6 you must include the date.

In Block 8 you must include the place.

In Block 12d. you must include the sum certain specific dollar amount of your claim.

Recognize that you will not be able to recover more than the amount stated in Block 12d. unless you can prove "newly discovered evidence not reasonably discoverable at the time of presenting the claim to the federal agency, or upon allegation and proof of intervening facts . . . ." 28 U.S.C. § 2675(b).

In Block 13a. you must sign the form.

If you are a representative of the claimant include evidence of your authority to present the claim.

3. Submit the written claim that includes a sum certain to the Federal agency that you believe is responsible for the tort. You may submit the claim by mail, courier service, or hand. If you are not sure which agency is responsible, submit the claim to each of the agencies that might be involved, but do so well in advance of the two-year anniversary of the claims accrual.

The Department of Justice regulations on administrative tort claims are attached at Appendix C.1.

APPENDIX H

Checklist for Filing FTCA Suit

1. Before you can file suit, you must first exhaust your administrative remedy by filing an administrative tort claim with the relevant Federal agency and waiting until either the agency denies the claim in writing or six months pass. 28 U.S.C. § 2675(a); *see* Appendix G.

2. You must file your suit in Federal district court no later than six months after the date of the agency's denial of your administrative claim. Otherwise your suit will be "forever barred." 28 U.S.C. § 2401(b).

3. You must file your Complaint in the United States District Court for either the Federal district in which you reside or the Federal district where the act or omission occurred. 28 U.S.C. § 1402(b).

4. You must properly effect service of process on the United States under Federal Rule of Civil Procedure 4(i)(1) by serving a copy of the Summons and Complaint on the United States Attorney for the Federal district where the action is pending **and** by sending a copy of the Summons and Complaint to the Attorney General of the United States by certified or registered mail.

The Attorney General's address is:

Attorney General of the United States
U.S. Department of Justice
950 Pennsylvania Avenue, NW
Washington, DC 20530-0001

Note that a plaintiff cannot serve process. Federal Rule of Civil Procedure 4(c)(2).

Table of Cases

Index